# BLACKJACK STRATEGY

*Also by Michael Benson*

Vintage Science Fiction Films
Ballparks of North America
Dream Teams
Who's Who In The JFK Assassination
Monster Trucks
Stock Car Spectacular
Pickup Trucks
Dale Earnhardt
Muscle Cars
Crashes & Collisions
Women in Racing
Convertibles
Gloria Estefan
Essential Bowling

# BLACKJACK STRATEGY

## Tips and Techniques for Beating the Odds

### MICHAEL BENSON
#### FOREWORD BY BERT RANDOLPH SUGAR

Printed in Canada

10 9 8 7 6 5 4 3 2 1

Library of Congress Cataloging-in-Publication Data

Benson, Michael.
    Blackjack strategy : tips and techniques for beating the odds / Michael Benson;
    foreword by Bert Randolph Sugar.
        p. cm.
    Includes bibliographical references.
    ISBN 1-58574-026-8
    1. Blackjack (Game)  I. Title.
GV1295.B55 B45 2000
795.4'23—dc21

                                                    00-027102

# DEDICATION

*To my Ol' Man*

# TABLE OF CONTENTS

# ACKNOWLEDGMENTS

The author wishes to thank the following persons and organizations: Jake Elwell; Enrica Gadler; Tony & Marie Grasso; Jackpot Junction Casino Hotel (Morton, MN); Eric Ketchum; Greig O'Brien; The Rio All-Suite Casino Resort (Las Vegas, NV); Bert Randolph Sugar; The Treasure Bay Casino (Biloxi, MS).

# FOREWORD

The game "21"—or Blackjack—is not all that difficult to understand. What most players don't understand is how to win at the game. There is a lot of misinformation out there, and few sure signs—such as the one in Las Vegas several years ago when a casino's neon sign went on the blink, literally, and for several embarrassing hours alternated between "WE NEVER CLOSE" and "WE NEVER _LOSE."

Most times, if you're a normal blackjack player, you're like the Siamese twins who, coming away from the table and being asked whether they had won, answered, "Yes and no!"

Because the true point of the exercise is winning, *Blackjack Strategy* provides a crucial education toward increasing your chances of answering "Yes." Michael Benson tells you your chances of winning, how to gauge your play versus the house, and, most important of all, lets you know for the first time—as playwright George S. Kaufman once told a bridge partner who had been misreading his cards all game and had asked permission to go to the men's room—"what you have in your hand."

Read this book, learn its lessons, and you too will be answering "Yes!" whenever someone asks you if you've won.

—Bert Randolph Sugar
Author, *The Caesar's Palace Sports Book of Betting*

# BLACKJACK STRATEGY

# INTRODUCTION

## COUNTING TO 21 WITHOUT GETTING ARRESTED FOR INDECENT EXPOSURE

There have been many books written over the years designed to make readers believe that, with the proper strategy, various games of chance can become lucrative pastimes. These books range from the mildly misleading to the ludicrous. Fill Your Pockets with Lottery Loot, Spin Your Way to Riches at the Roulette Wheel, Dice Are Nice, etc., etc., etc.

Sorry, no matter how much you study, you can't "win" at the lottery. Or the roulette wheel. Or the slot machines. These games are mathematically rigged against you, and there is nothing you can do to alter that. In fact, in some games—roulette, for example—the house advantage is as high as five percent, which means that for every $100 a player risks, he will lose an average of $5 to the house.

There is only one casino game in which a player, if he plays perfectly, can gain a mathematical advantage over the house. That game is blackjack. In other words, a really good blackjack player can win over the long run. This is not true of any other casino game offered. After learning the strategy and techniques taught in this book, the advantage can and will be yours.

Do not be intimidated by the amount of information in this book. The lessons that need to be learned are presented one at a time, and need not be absorbed all at once. First you will learn how to play, then how to minimize a casino's advantage through proper basic strategy. Once you are comfortable with these lessons, move to the next section which explains how and why card counting works and how to do it. Finally, you will be taught the effect card counting has on your basic strategy rules and how to manage your money to maximize your winnings.

Remember, take it slow . . . one step at a time—and by the time you finish you'll be a true master of blackjack.

## ABOUT THE GAME

A deck of 52 playing cards is a magical thing. The number, face, and suit possibilities create permutations and combinations of near-infinite proportions. The first playing cards were used in China, and the 52-card deck that we are familiar with comes from the seventeenth-century French. For a time, long after those cards had been adopted by the English, the deck was known as the "French pack."

The history of wagering is as old as man himself. We know that gambling was popular in Ancient China (24th century B.C.) and in the Greek Empire, but there is no reason to believe that either of those civilizations invented it. To gamble is to be human, and no doubt that was always the case.

Derived from the French card games "Chemin de Fer" and "Ferme," the first blackjack-like games were played in France in the early eighteenth century. These games merged and were standardized into a single game known as "Vingt-et-un" (21).

The first record of the game being played in North America comes from the early nineteenth century, but it was probably played sooner than that, no doubt coming over from England during the days of colonial America.

American casino gambling was first available to the men of the Old West. Wagering was legal in the Western Territories from the 1850s until 1910. For the next 21 years it was illegal to operate a house of chance. Then Nevada made gambling legal in 1931 and, well, you know what happened after that.

The game first became known as blackjack in the casinos of Las Vegas. Not the sprawling neon metropolis of the 21st century, but the young, savage Las Vegas—the Las Vegas of Bugsy Siegal. At first, the game was known as 21 but when it was initially offered it was not very popular. Poker and craps were the games of choice. In order to entice players to move over to the 21 table, the casinos sweetened the deal: a 21 hand that featured the Ace of Spades plus either the Jack of Clubs or the Jack of Spades would win a whopping ten-to-one on the player's bet.

The name blackjack stuck, long after casinos stopped paying the bonus. (The pay for a blackjack now is customarily three-to-two on a player's bet, no matter what color the Ace or the Ten.)

Blackjack came to the East Coast of the United States in 1978 when legalized gambling came to Atlantic City, New Jersey, a boardwalk town previously best known for the Miss America pageant and a horse that dove off a pier.

Since then, legalized gambling has become available in most regions of the country, largely on Native American reservations. Today casinos exist around the world.

These days, blackjack is the most popular table game in most casinos—and the reason is simple. It's an easy game to play. You don't need to be an expert to play blackjack. You only need to be an expert to play it well.

It wasn't until the 1950s that gamblers with slide rules began to take a serious look at blackjack and formulated a set of rules that would optimize a player's chances of winning.

The true father of card counting is Professor Edward O. Thorp who published a book called *Beat the Dealer,* in 1963. (Professor Thorp has since turned his attention to beating the stock market.) Thorp's book about blackjack so frightened casinos that the rules of the game were changed to make card counting more difficult. Still, the mathematicians have kept up with the casinos, and this book, if followed to the letter, offers state-of-the-art moves to win money at the blackjack table, no matter what the house rules are.

Because an advantage can be gained, one can consistently make money at blackjack. And that is simply not true of any other organized form of gambling. There can never be an animal known as a professional roulette player. There can never be a professional slot machine player. The more you play roulette, the more you play the slot machines, the more you will lose and that's a simple fact. But this is not necessarily true of blackjack.

There are professional blackjack players. The men (or, ever-increasingly, women) who actually make a living from playing 21 are not anything like they would be portrayed in a movie, however. They really exist, and they come in all shapes and sizes. Many look more like accountants than like secret agents—more like Joe Sixpack than James Bond.

For reasons we will soon discover, it is important that the professional blackjack player be inconspicuous. The more a pro can blend in with the scenery, the better off he is.

One such pro is an ordinary-looking thirty-year-old man we'll call Tim Churchill. Today he may be worth several million dollars—and he made every penny of it by playing blackjack. Tim's license plate reads, "ACE-TEN."

Churchill began playing blackjack when he was 17. It was love at first sight. He started with about $4,000 and lost all of it—but he was hooked. No longer content to play the game with the percentages in the house's favor, Tim stayed out of the casinos for a while (he had to, being broke), and he went to work.

Tim, a computer whiz, learned which moves to make and when. His technique, as you will learn, involves keeping a running ratio of the number of low cards compared to the number of high cards remaining to be dealt.

Through hard work and plenty of burning of the midnight oil, Tim earned the equivalent of a doctorate of blackjack. Now, a self-trained Phenom, he was ready for his comeback. He went back to the casino. He won steadily—and he has been winning ever since.

It is a sexy but lonely life.

"Women find it irresistible—at first," Churchill says. "But never for very long. They think it is going to be like in the movies, that I'll be a wild playboy—but to make money I have to work hard, long hours. The ladies get bored with it pretty quickly."

After a decade as a winning blackjack player, Churchill has been banned from most of the blackjack houses in both the United States and the United Kingdom.

"The only ones I'm not banned at are those where I haven't been yet—and since the casinos share information, I probably would be recognized there as well," Churchill says. "I have never thought the treatment I receive from casinos is fair. They treat me as if I were a card cheat, and I am not a cheat. I have merely come up with a method that works."

So what does he do? How does he continue to make a living?

"I only gamble three months out of the year now. The rest of the year I teach blackjack classes," he says. Sessions cost $500 apiece. "And, I've become a master of disguise," Churchill confesses. He has been an Asian Indian, a bleached-blond surfer dude, and even a little old lady, in dress and gray wig.

So, as you can see, if your goal is to become an expert blackjack player, a card counter who can regularly beat the house, it is not going to be clear sailing between you and becoming a millionaire. It is a long row to hoe, and the casinos, understandably, place as many obstacles in front of card counters as they can—including barring the door.

# CHAPTER ONE
# HOW TO PLAY

## SETTING THE SCENE

The dealer—or "croupier," if you are lucky enough to be playing in Monte Carlo—sits behind a table that is shaped like a semi-circle. Though some tables differ, there are seven seats for gamblers at a normal blackjack table.

When facing the dealer, the seat at the far right is known as "First Base." The player who sits there is sometimes referred to as the "First Baseman." The seat at the far left is called "Third Base." The player who takes that seat becomes the "Third Baseman."

Old wives will tell you that Third Base is the place to be, since a player sitting there has a better chance of winning. There is no mathematical justification for this, although some players do feel more comfortable, and therefore concentrate more effectively, when they go last.

Also, some players who count cards say that it is easiest for them to maintain their running count (you'll find out what that is later) when they are playing Third Base.

The cards are dealt clockwise from a plastic box called a "shoe," which contains a varying number of 52-card decks. The number of decks in the shoe depends on the casino and the table where you are playing.

A table is sometimes distinguished by the number of decks in its shoe. In some casinos all of the tables will have the same number of decks in their shoes. In both cases, tables will be further differentiated by the minimum and maximum bets that are allowed.

Each player has a small circle, or sometimes a box, marked in front of them on the cloth of the table. Before they are dealt cards, they must place their wager in chips inside the circle. No chips, no cards. If they lose, they lose their chips.

## IMPORTANT TIP

Once you have placed your bet, do not touch your chips. The dealer will think that you are attempting to cheat, and he will scold you immediately. Touching the chips after the bet has been placed is prohibited because some players will try to add or subtract chips after they see their cards, which is cheating.

If a player wins, his chips are doubled in value. If he gets a blackjack, an Ace and a card worth 10 points, most casinos pay back one-and-a-half times the player's bet.

A player starts with two cards. He may stay with those or be dealt additional cards as he wishes. To win, a player must accumulate more points than the dealer without going over 21. Remember—and this cannot be emphasized enough—no matter how many players are at the table, you are playing against the dealer.

If you bust, or go over 21, you lose immediately—even if the dealer later busts himself. It is not a push—that is, a tie, or a do-over—if both you and the dealer bust. You lose. (On the other hand, if you and the dealer have the same total, it is a push, or tie, and no money is won or lost.)

The dealer will always play the same way. He has to, bound by the rules. In most houses, the dealer has to stay if he has 17 or more, and he has to draw if he has 16 or less.

If you have more points than the dealer without going over 21, you win. It doesn't matter if another player has beaten you. He is playing against the dealer, and only the dealer, as well.

When the round, or hand, is over the cards are not put back into the deck, or shoe, but are instead pushed into a discard pile. The next round is dealt by the dealer from the remaining cards.

It is this rule of the game that makes the house beatable by a card counter. By counting which cards have already been used, a player can determine which cards are most likely to come up next.

We will be discussing card counting later on.

## LENGTH OF PLAY

You may play as long as you like, and you may stop playing at any time. You can start and stop playing as often as you like. Some players believe in playing only when "the table is hot" and watching the rest of the time.

I do not recommend playing for too long at any one stretch as, no matter how much coffee you drink, fatigue becomes a factor—and once you get blinky the house advantage skyrockets.

You also don't want to spend too long of a stretch at any one table. You don't want any of the dealers or other casino personnel to become too familiar with your style of play.

For reasons we will discuss more fully later on, the successful blackjack player is a nomad, a honey bee bopping from flower to flower, winning at one table and then moving on.

Some casinos allow players to play more than one hand at a time. Of course, that's a sign that the tables aren't full which might indicate—if you are playing in a region, on a day and at an hour when the casino should be crowded—that there is something wrong with the casino. Some casinos, you will learn if you keep your eyes and ears open along the strip, have acquired a reputation for having dealers that cheat, or casino personnel who are particularly irritating to players who win.

A word to the wise when it comes to calling it a day (or night): If you have been playing for a long time and you have a great many lower denomination chips, you might ask the dealer to "color up" your chips—that is, exchange the lower denomination chips for a smaller number of higher denomination chips. This will make life easier when you cash in your chips.

# VALUE OF THE CARDS

Cards Two through Ten are worth their face value in blackjack.

Jacks, Queens and Kings are worth 10.

Aces are the only cards that give you a choice. In blackjack each Ace is worth either one point (*hard* count) or eleven points (*soft* count)—depending on which is best for you.

# THE REAL DEAL

When each player has placed his bet in front of him, the dealer begins dealing the cards from the shoe. There are two methods of dealing blackjack. One is called the *Nevada Deal,* and the other is called the *London Deal.*

With the Nevada Deal, practiced in Las Vegas in one- or two-deck games, the dealer deals each player two cards face down, called *hole cards,* while dealing himself one card face up (an *up card*) and one card face down. Face-down dealing is also called a "pitch" game, as the cards are "pitched" face down to the players.

The London Deal is used in the United Kingdom and Europe—as well as in many casinos along the boardwalk in Atlantic City, New Jersey—as well as, confusingly enough, in multi-deck games in Nevada. These dealers deal all up cards to the players and one up card to themselves.

The dealers in London do not take a second card until all of the players at the table have completed their play. In both styles the best hand is called a blackjack, a combination of a card worth 10 points and an Ace—the Ace in this case being worth 11.

As we shall see, it is much harder to "count cards" when a game using the Nevada Deal is being played, which is why this is the method used in one- or two-deck games in Las Vegas.

## IMPORTANT TIP

If you are playing blackjack at a casino that uses the London deal, and you are receiving both of your cards face up, do not touch them. Casinos prohibit the touching of face cards because this helps keep cheaters from marking the cards, so you might be mistaken for a cheater by the dealer if you touch a card that is face up.

If the Nevada deal is in effect, you have to touch your cards or you would never know what your face-down card was. However, you are prohibited from touching that card with BOTH HANDS.

While we're on the subject, it is not a good idea to touch any of your cards, dealt face up or face down, any more than you have to, as card fiddlers will inevitably attract unwelcome scrutiny from the dealer and the casino employee in charge of the immediate area, known as the *pit boss*.

## HOW TO WIN

In both styles, if no one gets blackjack, the player or the dealer wins if their total is closest to 21 without going over. If, after receiving two cards, a player's total number of points is not near enough to 21 to win (or so he believes), he has the option of getting another card. This is called drawing or "taking a hit."

The player may continue to take additional cards to add to his total, as long as he does not surpass 21. In some casinos there is a rule that says, if you acquire five cards without going over 21 you win.

To tell the dealer that he wants to draw another card, when it is his turn, a player will say *"hit me"* and then brush or scratch at the table just behind your cards. Another signal is brushing your original two cards behind your bet.

The hand signals are actually required in most places and verbal requests alone are not accepted. This is because the surveillance cameras are always watching and record the player's style of play through video rather than audio.

If the player wants to stick with what he has, he says he will *"stand."* This, too, usually must be communicated to the dealer non-verbally—either by a right-to-left wave of the hand or by tucking your cards underneath your bet.

## DOUBLING DOWN

After you have received your first two cards you are given the option of doubling your bet—but in exchange for this, the house requires that you can only receive one more card.

There are some casinos in northern Nevada that only allow players with a 10 or 11 to do this. The practice is called *doubling down*. The ability to determine when you have enough of an advantage over the dealer to increase your bet is one of the key skills to making money at blackjack.

In most casinos a player is allowed to increase his bet anywhere up to double after receiving two cards. If a player increases his bet, but by less than double, this is called *doubling for less.*

I do not recommend doubling for less however. Just about any situation that warrants doubling down warrants doubling down for the maximum amount—that is, double.

### IMPORTANT TIP

When doubling down be sure to place your second bet alongside your first bet, and not on top of it. Placing the second stack on top of the first is prohibited and will earn you an instant reprimand from the dealer.

Stacking the doubling down bet on top of the original bet is one method a cheater might use to more than double his bet after he knows the quality of his hand, which is against the rules.

## SPLITTING

If a player's first two cards match (i.e. two Sevens), this rule, offered in most houses of chance, allows him to split those cards up and play two hands, thus doubling his bet on the round. In order to do this you turn your cards face up (unless they are face up already, of course) and tell the dealer that you want to split.

Thus, each Seven becomes the first card in a separate hand. The player must put up a bet of an equal amount to the original bet for the second hand. Less is not allowed.

If the player, in turn, receives another Seven to complete one of his two new hands, he may then split again so that he is now playing three bets, and a third bet of equal value to the first two must be wagered.

Most casinos allow a player to split up to four times per round. (In some casinos, players are also allowed to double down after splitting.) If the cards that are being split happen to be Aces, the player is allowed to add only one card to each hand. Most clubs do not allow the re-splitting of Aces. If the player receives a third Ace, that's it.

One negative to doubling down in this scenario is that, if a Ten is drawn (that is, a King, Queen, Jack, or Ten, all worth 10) to join one or both of the Aces, those hands are not blackjack—although they are worth 21 points. Therefore a player's hand of, say, Ace/Ten (after splitting Aces) will only tie a dealer's total of 21 (with more than two cards), even though it appears that the dealer has a regular 21 to the player's blackjack.

In addition, most casinos allow splitting any two cards worth 10 points. That is, you can split a Queen and a Jack, or a Ten and a King. The reason is that this is a very poor play by the player, so they'll let you do it. (Very nice of them.) Never split Tens (or 10-value cards). You have a hand worth 20 points. Stick!

In all North American blackjack games players lose only their original bets if the dealer has blackjack. All split and doubling down bets are returned to the players. In most casinos, however, the dealer checks to see if he has black-jack before the players have an opportunity to split or double down.

# TAKING OUT INSURANCE

Insurance, sometimes known as betting for the dealer, is a side bet, completely independent of the bet you have made on your hand. This strategy is only offered when the dealer has an Ace showing.

By taking out insurance, you are betting that the dealer has blackjack. If he does have blackjack, your insurance chips are tripled—that is, paid off at two-to-one. If the dealer does not have blackjack, your insurance bet is lost.

The insurance bet cannot be more than half of the bet you made on your hand. You are allowed to bet less than half of the bet on your hand when you are taking out insurance, but any situation that warrants taking out insurance warrants taking it out in the maximum amount allowed.

If you are playing using the basic strategy of the game (charts for which can be found in the rear of this book), it is never a good idea to take out insurance. The bet only becomes a good one when you are counting cards and your True Count is plus three or greater. (You will understand what that means soon enough.)

Insurance is offered by the dealer before he checks his hole card to see if he has blackjack, lest he give it away—or "tell"—by some facial expression. After insurance bets are taken, or not, the dealer checks to see if he has blackjack. If the dealer does have blackjack, all players who don't also have blackjack lose, those that do have blackjack get a push (a tie), and those that took out insurance are paid two-to-one on their side bet.

The player who takes out insurance to the maximum amount will break even—even if his hand is not a blackjack but the dealer's is. His original bet will be lost but the half bet on the side will be tripled to compensate. This is sometimes referred to as "even money."

If the player also has blackjack and has taken out insurance, he wins money. The bet he made on his hand is a push and his insurance bet is paid off at two-to-one.

Many dealers will tell players that they should always take out insurance when they have blackjack and the dealer has an Ace showing because "you can't lose." Well, true enough—but in the long run playing this way will diminish the amount that you win. That won't do. We're trying to make a living here.

## SURRENDER AND EARLY SURRENDER

Say you find yourself in a bleak situation. You have been dealt a Nine and a Seven, for a total of 16. The dealer has a Ten showing. If you take a hit the chances are good that you will go over 21 and bust.

If you stand pat the chances are good that the dealer's other card is better than a six so that he beats you. The game provides such a glum player a way to cut his losses.

You can *surrender* right then and there. When you do this you lose only half of your bet as long as the dealer does not have blackjack. There are times when surrendering is a good way to go.

There are some casinos that now offer a rule known as *early surrender,* which allows the surrendering player to keep half his bet *regardless* of whether or not the dealer has blackjack.

# THE HOUSE ADVANTAGE

Assuming that you are playing blackjack at an equal level of skill with the dealer, the dealer still stands to win one to three percent more frequently than you. This is because he gets to go last.

You always have to decide to stay or take a card before the dealer. If you decide to take a card and your total goes over 21, you lose—and the dealer never had to make a decision.

Even if there is more than one player against the dealer, and—after you've taken one card too many—the dealer eventually busts, you still lose. Beating the dealer, I can't repeat enough, is the name of the game.

You never get that advantage. There are no "changing sides" or "alternating serves" in blackjack. The dealer is always the dealer. That's how the casinos make money.

Given the standardized rules under which dealers must play (must hit a hard 16 but stand on a hard 17) mathematical research shows the dealer will bust less than 30 times per 100 hands.

Studies have shown that the dealer will deal himself a natural 21 five times over that same span and will acquire 21 with three or more cards seven times. In the great majority of hands, about 60%, the dealer will finish with a count of 17, 18, 19, or 20.

# PROBABILITY OF BUSTING

Blackjack, as you can see, is a game of probabilities, and the primary probability a player has to determine is the probability of busting.

For example, if you hold a hand that adds up to 15, and there is no Ace in it, what are the chances of you busting if you take a hit (assuming that all hands are being dealt from a fresh shoe)?

Obviously, the more total points you have in your initial two-card hand, the greater the chances you will bust if you ask the dealer for an additional card.

The chart below shows the percentage of times you will bust if you take a hit when starting with a given hand. Returning to our earlier question, you'll see that, if you hold a 15 and take a hit on 100 occasions, you will bust 58 times.

YOUR HAND (HARD)

| 11 (and below) | 12 | 13 | 14 | 15 | 16 | 17 | 18 | 19 | 20 | 21 |
|---|---|---|---|---|---|---|---|---|---|---|
| % BUSTS IF HIT 0% | 31 | 39 | 56 | 58 | 62 | 69 | 77 | 85 | 92 | 100% |

# CHAPTER TWO
# MINIMIZING YOUR DISADVANTAGE: BASIC STRATEGY

## WINNING STRATEGIES

Here are some simple rules involving when to draw a card and when to stand, when to double down and when to split pairs. There are not many things in life that you have to memorize, but—if you don't want to lose the rent money at the blackjack table—this set of rules is one of them. (Multiplication tables are another, but you knew that.)

The following strategies are based on Atlantic City rules (see Chapter Six, Casino Specifics). If you're saying, "Hey, but I'm not IN Atlantic City, dude," well, don't worry. Basic strategies for different sets of rules are available in the set of 40 charts at the back of this book.

Note that in this section all Tens, Jacks, Queens, and Kings are referred to as Tens, as this is their numerical value.

Once you see the dealer's up card and have looked at your own initial two cards, you should ask yourself the following questions IN THIS ORDER:

1) Do I surrender?
2) If I have pairs, do I split them? (If you split a pair, start this flow again for each new hand.)
3) Do I double down?
4) Do I hit or stick?

The basic strategy rules below will tell you what to do.

There are two basic sets of rules for standing and drawing. One set is for when you have an Ace in your hand and you are counting it as a value of 11—what they call a soft hand.

The other set is for "hard hands"—that is hands that have no Ace, or an Ace that is being counted as one. Always count an Ace as 11 first, (consider the soft hand first), and only count the Ace as a value of one after your total exceeds 21 when counting the ace as 11. (You can never bust by hitting a "soft hand." If you go over 21, then you change the value of your Ace from 11 to one, and now the hand is a "hard hand.")

Remember: Before deciding if you should hit or stand on either a hard or a soft hand, you must first determine if doubling down, splitting or surrendering is called for.

We will start with the rules for hard hands.

# STANDING AND DRAWING: HARD HAND

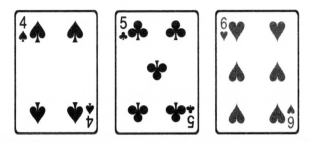

**If the dealer is showing a Four, Five, or Six, and your cards total 12 or more, STAND. If your total is 11 or less, DRAW.**

If we always assume that the next card is going to be worth 10—since there are more cards worth 10 than any other kind—we quickly see that these situations give us an opportunity to make the dealer's limitations work against him.

If our total is 12 or more and we draw a Ten, we bust. If the dealer has a Six showing, the most common total he will have in his hand is 16—and that means that he has to take another card, which we still assume is a Ten. Thus, the dealer will bust, and you will win with your seemingly mediocre 12.

Of course, this will not happen every time—just more often than anything else. Card counters, who know ahead of time that there are, percentage-wise, more Tens in the deck than there were when the shoe was freshly shuffled, can be even more confident when betting that the dealer will bust showing a Six if you have 12 and stand.

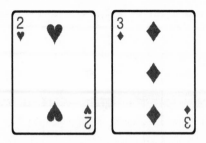

**If the dealer is showing a Two or a Three, and your cards total 13 or more, STAND. If your total is 12 or less, DRAW.**

Now that you've learned the rule about always assuming the next card is a Ten, here is the exception to it. We draw on a 12 in this situation because the dealer will successfully beat our 12 with a Two or a Three showing more frequently than we will bust if we draw.

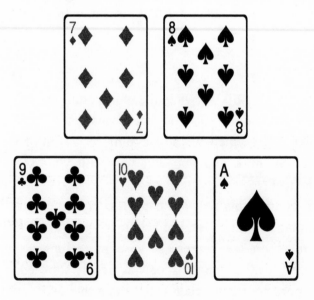

**If the dealer is showing a Seven, Eight, Nine, Ten, or an Ace, and your cards total 17 or more, STAND. If your cards total 16 or less, DRAW.**

This final rule is the hardest for the player to believe. An inexperienced player who holds a hard 16 will not want to take a hit if the dealer has a crummy card like a Seven or an Eight showing. The player can only think in the short term, extremely short term, and he resists this move because of the high frequency of busting.

Still, study after study has shown that this is the play that gives you the greatest chance of winning. You may bust frequently, but in the long run taking another card beats the dealer with a Seven up more often than standing does.

If you have a hard 17, always stand. Hitting a 16 is difficult, but sometimes it needs to be done. A player who has 16 against a dealer's Ten is almost always going to lose, but he will lose less frequently if he takes a hit than if he stands.

## STANDING AND DRAWING: SOFT HAND

The rules that follow assume that you are counting your Ace as 11 points. Once again, these strategies are to be used only after you have determined whether or not to split, double down or surrender.

The risk of busting is nil when you have a soft hand because, if your total goes over 21, you count your Ace as one instead of 11 and refigure your total as a hard hand.

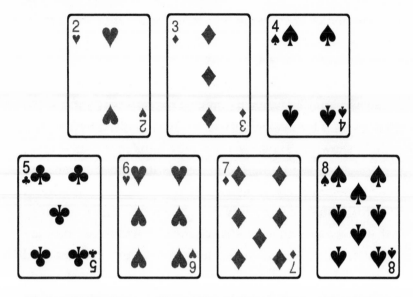

If the dealer has a Two, Three, Four, Five, Six, Seven, or Eight showing, and your cards total 18 or more, STAND. If your cards total 17 or less, DRAW.

If the dealer has a Nine, Ten, or Ace showing, and your cards total 19 or more, STAND. If your cards total 18 or less, DRAW.

REMEMBER: Always stand on a hard 17 and draw on a soft 17. There is no error in blackjack made more often than that of a player standing on a soft 17, when taking a hit is the correct play.

**Only stick on soft hands which total 18 or better—unless the dealer is showing a Nine, Ten, or an Ace, in which case stick on soft hands which total 19 or better.**

Here's an example: You get dealt Ace, Five for a total of 16 (this is a "soft 16" with the Ace equaling 11). You hit and get a Seven. Now you have a "hard 13" (Ace, Five, Seven with the Ace equaling one). If you hit and get a Three, you now you have a "soft 19" (Ace, Five, Three with the Ace equaling 11).

## WHEN TO DOUBLE DOWN WITH A HARD HAND

As we explained earlier, you are allowed to increase your bet up to double after seeing your original two cards. This is called doubling down, and after doing so, you are allowed to draw only one more card.

**If your cards total 12 or more, do not double down.**

**If you are playing a game in which the dealer stands when he holds a soft 17, and your cards total 11, double down unless the dealer is showing an Ace. If you are playing outside Atlantic City and your dealer must take a hit when he holds a soft 17, then double down if you have 11 no matter what the dealer is showing.**

Any Ten gives you 21. This is a very strong hand.

**If your cards total 10, double down—unless the dealer has a Ten or an Ace showing.**

In other words, you want to double down here only when your 10 gives you the advantage, as it would not if the dealer were indicating a very strong hand with a Ten or Ace showing.

**If your cards total nine, and the dealer has a Three, Four, Five, or Six showing, double down.**

**If your cards total nine and the dealer has a Two, Seven, Eight, Nine, Ten, or Ace showing, do not double down.**

**If your cards total eight or less, do not double down.**

## WHEN TO DOUBLE DOWN WITH A SOFT HAND

**If you have two Aces, do not double down** (unless there is a house rule that prohibits splitting Aces, in which case you double down only if the dealer has a Five or a Six showing).

**If you have an Ace and a Two (Soft 13), or an Ace and a Three (Soft 14), double down only if the dealer has a Five or a Six showing.**

If you have an Ace and a Four (Soft 15), or an Ace and a Five (Soft 16), double down only if the dealer has a Four, Five, or Six showing.

If you have an Ace and a Six (Soft 17), or an Ace and a Seven (Soft 18), double down only if the dealer is showing a Three, Four, Five, or Six. (If the dealer hits a soft 17, and you have a Soft 18, you would also double down if the dealer is showing a Two.)

## WHEN TO SPLIT PAIRS

As you recall, when you are dealt a pair—that is, two Twos, two Threes or two Tens—you are allowed to split them, thus creating two separate hands.

You are required to place a bet on the second hand equal to your original bet. The two hands are then played separately so that you may win both, lose both or win one and lose one to break even. (In some casinos you may also double down after splitting.)

Splitting is done most frequently when the dealer has a low card showing. With the dealer indicating a poor hand we want to maximize our bet.

When the dealer has a high card, he has a strong hand, we are likely to lose, so we want to minimize our risk. So, here are the rules when playing on the Boardwalk as to when the odds say you should split your hand. Again, for variations depending on different casino rules see the charts at the back of the book.

**If you have a Pair of Twos, a Pair of Threes, or a Pair of Sevens, split them if the dealer is showing a Two, Three, Four, Five, Six, or Seven. Do not split them if the dealer is showing an Eight, Nine, Ten, or Ace.**

**If you have a Pair of Fours, split them only if the dealer is showing a Five or Six.**

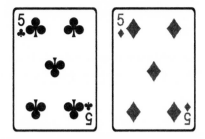

**NEVER split a Pair of Fives or a Pair of Tens.**

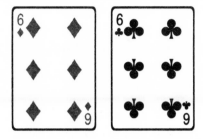

**If you have a Pair of Sixes, split them if the dealer is showing a Two, Three, Four, Five, or Six. Do NOT split them if the dealer is showing a Seven, Eight, Nine, Ten, or Ace.**

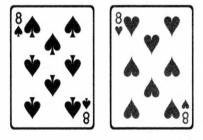

**Split a Pair of Eights, unless the dealer is showing a Ten or an Ace. In those two cases, surrender.** These are cut-your-losses moves since you've been dealt a hard 16. Yuck. Might as well take your chances of getting at least one 18 out of the round and break even.

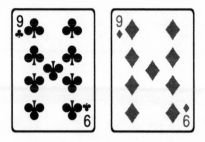

**Split a Pair of Nines unless the dealer is showing a Seven, Ten, or Ace.** (There is an old saying around casinos that you don't split nines when the dealer is showing a nine, but this is a myth.) You don't split up your Nines against a dealer's Seven because you have 18, and, if the dealer draws a Ten, he only has 17.

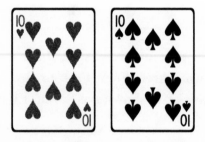

**NEVER split Tens.** You already have 20. Your chances of winning are already very strong.

**ALWAYS split a pair of Aces**—unless, of course, the house prohibits the splitting of Aces. Houses that do allow the splitting of Aces usually allow only one additional card to be drawn on top of those Aces, but it makes no difference. It is still the intelligent play no matter what card the dealer had showing.

## WHEN TO SURRENDER

We discussed surrendering earlier. This rule gives you the option of giving up after you see your initial two cards. You get half of your bet back to risk on a better hand. You cannot surrender, however, if the dealer has blackjack.

**When the dealer has an Ace showing, SURRENDER if you are holding 13, 14, 15, or 16.**

**When the dealer has a Ten showing, SURRENDER if you have a 14, 15, or 16—unless your 16 is comprised of a Pair of Eights, in which case split.**

When the dealer has a Nine showing, SURRENDER if you have a 16—unless it is a pair, in which case split.

If you are lucky and have an opportunity to play a one-deck game, you should also surrender if you are dealt a pair of Sevens and the dealer is showing a Ten.

## WHEN TO EARLY SURRENDER

If early surrender—a surrender that is allowed regardless of whether the dealer has blackjack—is an available strategy at your table, here are the correct times to exercise that option:

**EARLY SURRENDER if the dealer has an Ace showing and you are holding a hard five, six, seven, 12, 13, 14, 15, 16, or 17.**

**EARLY SURRENDER if the dealer has a Ten showing and you are holding a hard 14, 15, or 16.**

## CHANGES IN BASIC STRATEGY WHEN PLAYING ONE- OR TWO-DECK GAMES

If doubling down is permitted after splitting, add to your basic strategy these instances when splitting is advised:

When you have a pair of Sevens, also SPLIT if the dealer is showing an Eight.

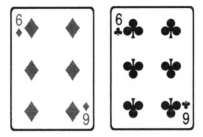

When you have a pair of Sixes, also SPLIT if the dealer is showing a Seven.

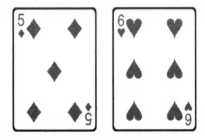

Also DOUBLE DOWN if you have 11 and the dealer is showing an Ace.

Also DOUBLE DOWN when you have 9 and the dealer is showing a Two.

Okay, we have discussed the rules of basic strategy, the moves that will absolutely minimize the house advantage. Be warned: playing this basic strategy will not give you an advantage over the house (the only way to have an advantage is by counting cards) BUT, it is statistically the best strategy and will reduce your disadvantage to the range of −.50 percent to −.18 percent, depending on the number of decks and the specific rules under which you are playing.

# CHAPTER THREE
# GAINING AN
# ADVANTAGE:
# COUNTING CARDS

I know what you're thinking: "Sure, there are geniuses with photographic memories out there who may be able to count cards during a blackjack game, but I will never be able to do it."

This insecurity is based on a common misconception among blackjack novices. You do not have to remember the exact value of every card you have seen—although that would give you a great advantage if you could.

And remember, you NEVER have to remember the suit of a card. Despite the name of the game, there is no difference in the value of a Black Jack over a Red Jack—or the Ten of Diamonds, for that matter.

Another misconception that tends to discourage the curious newcomer: There is no card-counting system that will allow you to win every round. By counting cards you are merely shifting the odds so that you will win more money than you lose—and thus make money—over the long run! You don't necessarily do this by winning more hands but rather by betting more when you win and less when you lose.

Card counters further increase the odds of winning more money than they lose through what is known as *bet sizing*— that is, by increasing or lowering their bets depending on the ratios they are keeping in their head.

Indeed, a player who *flat bets,* that is bets the same amount on each hand, is admitting that he is not a card counter. A fellow who bets that way is using the basic strategy—if he is using any strategy at all.

Even before blackjack players figured out how to count cards they knew that betting big "when the cards were hot," and small when they were cold, was one way to overcome the house advantage.

Much of basic strategy is based on assuming the next card is always a Ten, since there are more Tens—that is, cards worth 10—than any other kind. If we keep track of the ratio of Tens to cards unlikely to make the dealer bust, we can gear the size of our bet to our degree of certainty.

Remember again, our probability of winning starts out slightly less than 50 percent. By following the usage of the cards out of the shoe, we can push that to slightly above 50 percent.

But that—if you play blackjack intelligently over the long run—is the difference between making money and losing money. Expert card counters increase their chances of winning by something less than two percent, but that is all they need to make a living, if they can get in enough hours at the table—or bet big enough.

# HOW TO KEEP A RUNNING COUNT

A card counter assigns a value to a type of card to make it easy to count. In other words, if a player designates that cards worth Ten will, in his system, equal $-1$, he will subtract one from his count each time he sees a Ten.

The player then designates that the small cards, cards Two through Six in most systems, are worth +1. He adds a one for each card of that type he sees. Those +1s and $-1$s are known as *card weight*. The Sevens, Eights, and Nines are ignored.

You are only concerned with the specific total of your own hand and the dealer's hand. The other players' hands are converted by you into card weights. The running number, or *count,* in your head will be either above zero or below zero, thus telling the player the ratio between high and low cards remaining in the deck.

| CARD | WEIGHT |
|------|--------|
| 2 | +1 |
| 3 | +1 |
| 4 | +1 |
| 5 | +1 |
| 6 | +1 |
| 7 | 0 |
| 8 | 0 |
| 9 | 0 |
| 10 | $-1$ |
| Jack | $-1$ |
| Queen | $-1$ |
| King | $-1$ |
| Ace | $-1$ |

You may say, "Isn't that backwards? If you like the high cards and don't like the little ones, shouldn't the big ones be plus and the little ones minus?" The answer is no, for the simple reason that we are not keeping track of the cards that have been played. We are keeping track of the cards that are left in the shoe.

## TRUE COUNT

When playing a one-deck game, the running count was enough for a card counter to maximize his earnings. But the casinos smartened up to card counters very quickly and changed the rules.

The number one anti-card counting strategy implemented by the casinos was the introduction of multi-pack blackjack games. The running count was no longer enough because each card represented a smaller percentage of all the cards.

The games, which now featured as many as six or eight decks, became impossible for dealers to manage without the use of a box called a shoe.

If our running count is plus 10 and there is only one deck of cards (52 cards) left in the shoe, we have a much stronger advantage over the dealer than we would if we had the same running count but there were four decks left in the shoe. But how much greater? The math whizzes went to work. Soon a mathematical formula to adjust to the extra cards was invented.

The key was to find a formula that adapted the running count to the number of cards that were left in the shoe. The running count needed to be adapted into the True Count. This is how they did it:

They divided the running count by the number of decks (or fraction of a deck) remaining to be dealt. Therefore, if the running count is plus 10 and there is one deck left in the shoe, then the True Count remains plus 10. However, if there are four decks left in the shoe and the running count is plus 10, then the True Count becomes only plus two and a half. If there are two decks left in the shoe, then the True Count is plus five. If there are three decks left, then the True Count is plus 3.3, which you could keep in your head as "greater than three."

Be aware that True Count conversion works a little differently if you are playing a one-deck game. You are always dealing with a fraction of a deck. If your running count is plus four and you have one-half of a deck left to be dealt, then you divide one-half into four and you get plus eight. Remember, when you divide a whole number by a fraction the result becomes larger rather than smaller. So the formula holds true, but the resulting number, the True Count, grows instead of shrinks from the running count.

If the running count is minus one and there is one-third of a deck remaining to be dealt, then you would divide one-third into minus one and get minus three. This is the reason why all card-counting blackjack players would rather play in a one- or two-deck game. Very large advantages and disadvantages can be ascertained by counting cards when there is less than a deck remaining to be dealt.

(I should note here that there are conversion formulae to adapt a running count into a True Count that are a zillion times more complicated than this, and they may better fine tune your system to a small degree, but for someone who is first learning to count cards, this method is sufficient and certainly more than erases the house advantage.)

## HOW TO TELL THE NUMBER OF DECKS REMAINING IN THE SHOE

To estimate the number of decks remaining to be dealt, glance at the discard rack. Don't stare. There is only one reason to scrutinize the discard rack and it is discouraged heavily by the casinos. Glance casually.

If it is a six-deck shoe and the discard rack is half filled, then there are approximately three decks left in the shoe. For the novice, it is not necessary to be more precise than this.

## YOU DON'T HAVE TO BE A GENIUS

We asked a professional blackjack player what he would say to beginners who were intimidated by the thought of counting cards. He offered us, as professional blackjack players are wont to do, an analogy:

"Counting the cards is like counting how many people are in a room when you are outside the room, and all you can see is the entrance and the exit," said the pro. "Three people go in, two people come out—that's plus one (+1). Then two go in and one goes out (+2). Then one goes in and one comes out at the same time, so you ignore it (still +2). Then a couple goes in and at the same time another couple goes out, so you ignore that too (still +2). Simple!

"The Two, Three, Four, Five, and Six cards are the people going in. The Ten, Jack, Queen, King, and Ace are the people going out. And the count (+2) is how many more large cards than small ones are left in the deck."

Some blackjack experts have suggested that the best way to learn counting is to get into it gradually, such as by only counting the Fives and Aces. Aces are minus one and Fives are plus one.

I don't recommend this. First of all, the information offered by counting only Fives and Aces is very small. All of the Fives could be out of the shoe and there still could be an excess of small cards in there.

Besides, the wait between cards that you count can be so long that you forget the count. As you practice, you'll find that the thing that makes counting cards easy is that it is a running count. The number is constantly fluctuating at the forefront of your mind, where you are very unlikely to forget it.

# EARS TO THE GOOD TIMES

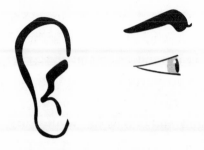

One of the ways dealers catch counters is by watching the players' eyes. (Some card counters always wear a baseball cap when they play blackjack so that the direction of their eyes cannot be picked up by the surveillance cameras and perhaps by the dealer as well.) The counter usually has to see every card that is visible. Someone who is concerned solely with basic strategy is more apt to keep focused only on his own cards and the dealer's.

But, believe it or not, there are some casinos along the boardwalk in Atlantic City where, because there are no hole cards, the dealers say the name of the card when they deal it.

This is music to the eyes of weary card counters. Players who want to count cards don't even have to move their eyes away from their own cards. They merely have to listen as the dealer says, "Three of Spades, King of Hearts. Seven of Diamonds, Ace of Hearts, etc."

# CHAPTER FOUR
# HOW CARD
# COUNTING AFFECTS
# BASIC STRATEGY

It is important to take these things one step at a time. If you try to learn too much at once, and don't adjust to your new knowledge gradually in the casino in action, then you are liable to be thinking about too many things at once, telegraphing your intentions and having a miserable time to boot.

It is better for you to become proficient at counting cards—a simple plus one, minus one system—even before you worry about adjusting for the True Count. And I would certainly recommend that you get comfortable with counting cards—surreptitiously, of course—before you worry about the ways in which the True Count can affect your basic strategy.

Of course, the easiest and most effective way to use card counting is to use your True Count merely to determine the size of your bet. Bet half when your count is in the minus numbers; your normal bet when the number is at zero, plus one or plus two; twice the normal amount if the count is plus three or greater; and four times your normal bet when the True Count meets or exceeds plus five—which is not to be confused with doubling down, a strategy you determine only after seeing your hand.

The trouble with altering your bet to suit your running count is that players who do not count cards do not usually bet that way. Therefore altering the size of your bet depending on the situation before you've seen your cards can lead the dealer to only one conclusion. You are counting cards.

There are instances when the correct play, whether to double down, whether to split, or simply whether or not to take a hit are affected by the True Count.

Therefore, a more subtle method of using the running count has been devised. This method alters facets of the basic strategy itself—whether to draw or stand, split or double down—depending on count.

So, if you have achieved this level of expertise, converting the running count into a True Count as you play, let's take a look at some of the ways that the True Count will change the basic strategy that we memorized earlier.

It has been determined that 87 percent of the advantage card counters get is by altering the size of their bet. Only the remaining 13 percent comes from changes in basic strategy caused by the True Count.

Say your True Count is deep in the negative numbers, indicating that a lot of the high cards have already been played. A disproportionate number of small cards remain in the shoe, and the dealer shows a Nine. *Do not double down.*

Say you have a True Count that is in the negative numbers and the dealer has a Four up while you're looking at a total of 12. Ordinarily this would be a time to stand, but, knowing that the remaining cards are low on high cards, take a hit.

Whenever the shoe is rich with low cards, bet low. This is when the house advantage is at its strongest. That's because a bad hand for the dealer is salvageable during a negative True Count. When the True Count is up into the positive numbers and there are more high cards in the shoe, the players' ability to stand on a 15 or a 16, while the dealer is obligated to hit those numbers, gives the player an advantage, because the dealer is more apt to bust. Therefore, the higher into the positive numbers your True Count gets the more you want to bet.

The variations in play—that is, changes in basic strategy—listed below are those used when the True Count is between minus two and

## NINE RULES OF THUMB

If the True Count is minus one or less:

Take a hit when you are holding 13 against a dealer's Two or Three.

If the True Count is plus two or greater:

Stand when holding 12 against a dealer's Two or Three.

Stand when holding 16 against a dealer's Ten.

Double down when holding 11 against a dealer's Ace.

Double down when holding eight against a dealer's Six.

If the True Count is plus three or greater:

Buy insurance. (This is the most important play variation of all.)

Double down when holding 10 against the dealer's Ace.

Double down when holding nine against a dealer's Two.

Double down when holding eight against a dealer's Five or Six.

plus five. When the True Count runs below minus two, players should stick to their basic strategy and bet their minimum amount. Times when the True Count runs greater than plus five are rare. When it happens, use your basic strategy and bet the maximum amount.

All of the variations in strategy based on the True Count listed below are based on Atlantic City rules (more than two decks being used, doubling down allowed on any hand, doubling down after splitting is allowed, and the dealer must stand when he holds a soft 17).

Eighteen of the play variations listed below are marked with an asterisk (*). Memorize these first, as they account for a full three-quarters of the advantage attained through play variation based on True Count.

## INSURANCE

**\*If your True Count is plus three or greater, buy insurance.**

## STANDING AND HITTING: HARD HANDS

**\*If the dealer has a Ten showing, and you are holding a hard 16, you would normally hit. But, if the True Count is more than zero, stand.**

*If the dealer has a Ten showing, and you are holding a hard 15, you would normally take a hit. But, if your True Count is plus five or greater, stand.

*If the dealer has a Nine showing, and you have a hard 16, you would normally take a hit. But, if the True Count is more than zero, stand.

*If the dealer has a Four or a Six showing, and you have a hard 12, you would normally stand. But, if your True Count is less than zero, take a hit.

*If the dealer has a Five showing, and you have a hard 12, you would normally stand. But, if your True Count is less than minus one, take a hit.

*If the dealer has a Three showing, and you have a hard 12, you would normally take a hit. But, if your True Count is plus two or greater, stand.

*If the dealer has a Two showing, and you have a hard 12, you would normally take a hit. But, if your True Count is plus three or more, stand.

*If the dealer has a Two showing, and you have a hard 13, you would normally stand. But, if your True Count is less than zero, take a hit.

*If the dealer has a Three showing, and you have a hard 13, you would normally stand. But, if your True Count is less than minus one, take a hit.

## STANDING AND HITTING: SOFT HANDS

If the dealer has an Ace showing, and you have a soft 18, you would normally hit. But, if your True Count is more than plus one, stand.

## DOUBLING DOWN: HARD HANDS

*If the dealer has an Ace showing, and you have a hard 11, you would normally take a hit. But, if your True Count is plus one or more, double down.

\*If the dealer has a Ten or an Ace showing, and you have a hard 10, you would normally take a hit. But, if your True Count is plus four or more, double down.

\*If the dealer has a Nine showing, and you have a hard 10, you would normally double down. But, if your True Count is less than minus one, take a hit.

\*If the dealer has a Two showing, and you have a hard nine, you would normally take a hit. But, if your True Count is plus one or more, double down.

*If the dealer has a Three showing, and you have a hard nine, you would normally double down. But, if your True Count is zero or less, take a hit.

If the dealer has a Four showing, and you have a hard nine, you would normally double down. But, if your True Count is minus two or less, take a hit.

*If the dealer has a Seven showing, and you have a hard nine, you would normally take a hit. But, if your True Count is plus three or more, double down.

If the dealer has a Six showing, and you have a hard eight, you would normally take a hit. But, if your True Count is plus one or more, double down. (Split if you have a Pair of Fours.)

If the dealer has a Five showing, and you have a hard eight, you would normally take a hit. But, if your True Count is plus three or greater, double down. (Split if you have a Pair of Fours.)

## DOUBLING DOWN: SOFT HANDS

If the dealer has a Six showing, and you have a soft 20 (that is, an Ace and a Nine), you would normally stand. But, if your True Count is plus four or more, double down.

If the dealer has a Five or a Six showing, and you have a soft 19 (Ace and Eight), you would normally stand. But, if your True Count is plus one or more, double down.

If the dealer has a Four showing, and you have a soft 19 (Ace, Eight), you would normally stand. But, if your True Count is plus three or more, double down.

If the dealer has a Two showing, and you have a soft 18 (Ace, Seven), you would normally stand. But, if your True Count is more than zero, double down.

If the dealer has a Three showing, and you have a soft 18 (Ace, Seven), you would normally double down. But, if your True Count is less than minus two, take a hit.

If the dealer has a Two showing, and you have a soft 17 (Ace, Six), you would normally take a hit. But, if the True Count is plus one or more, double down.

If the dealer has a Four showing, and you have a soft 16 (Ace, Five), you would normally double down. But, if your True Count is less than minus two, take a hit.

If the dealer has a Three showing, and you have a soft 16 (Ace, Five), you would normally take a hit. But, if your True Count is plus four or more, double down.

If the dealer has a Four showing, and you have a soft 15 (Ace, Four), you would normally double down. But, if your True Count is less than zero, take a hit.

If the dealer has a Four showing, and you have a soft 14 (Ace, Three), you would normally take a hit. But, if your True Count is plus one or more, double down.

If the dealer has a Five showing, and you have a soft 14 (Ace, Three), you would normally double down. But, if your True Count is less than minus one, take a hit.

If the dealer has a Four showing, and you have a soft 13 (Ace, Two), you would normally take a hit. But, if your True Count is plus three or greater, double down.

If the dealer has a Five showing, and you have a soft 13 (Ace, Two), you would normally double down. But, if your True Count is less than zero, take a hit.

If the dealer has a Six showing, and you have a soft 13 (Ace, Two), you would normally double down. But, if your True Count is less than minus one, take a hit.

## SPLITTING PAIRS

*If the dealer has a Six showing, and you are holding a Pair of Tens, you would normally stick. But, if your True Count is plus four or more, split.

*If the dealer has a Five showing, and you are holding a Pair of Tens, you would normally stick. But, if your True Count is plus five or more, split.

If the dealer has a Two showing, and you are holding a Pair of Nines, you would normally split. But, if your True Count is less than minus two, stand.

If the dealer has a Seven or an Ace showing, and you are holding a Pair of Nines, normally you would stick. But, if your True Count is plus three or more, split.

If the dealer has a Two showing and you are holding a Pair of Sixes, you would normally split. But, if your True Count is less than minus one, take a hit.

If the dealer has a Four showing, and you are holding a Pair of Fours, you would normally take a hit. But, if your True Count is plus one or more, split.

If the dealer has a Five showing and you are holding a Pair of Fours, you would normally split. But, if your True Count is less than minus one, take a hit.

If the dealer has an Eight showing, and you are holding a Pair of Threes, you would normally take a hit. But, if your True Count is plus four or more, split.

# CHAPTER FIVE
# MONEY MANAGEMENT

We have talked about how to handle your cards. Now let's talk about how to handle your money, which is every bit as important. Card counting does effect basic strategy now and again, but its true value comes as a governor to money management. As we have discussed, in general terms, card counting is best used to determine the size of your bet on a given hand. Now we will get down to specifics.

## RUNNING COUNT AND HOW MUCH YOU BET

Assuming that one dollar represents the smallest bet you plan to make and four dollars represents the maximum bet you plan to make, here is a money management strategy. Remember, it doesn't make any difference what cards you will be dealt or what card the dealer has showing because the decision of how much you are going to bet on the hand has to be made before a single card is dealt.

1) If your True Count is plus one or lower bet one dollar.
2) If the count is plus two or more, bet two dollars.
3) If you win your two-dollar bet, take the four dollars you receive and bet it, as long as your running count has remained at plus two or above.
4) Continue betting four-dollar hands as long as the count remains above plus two.

## THINGS TO DETERMINE BEFORE YOU START

1) Decide beforehand how much money you are willing to lose.
2) Decide how many times you want to play in the casino. (How long is your trip?)
3) Divide the amount of money by the number of times you want to play to determine the maximum amount you are willing to lose for each session. *Never lose more than this per session! Walk away!*

## UP SIDE MONEY MANAGEMENT

Decide beforehand how much winnings you will be satisfied with, for example, "If I buy $100 worth of chips, I will be satisfied if I walk away up $300." (*This does not mean that you walk away when you are up $300!*) You never want to limit your winnings. Only limit your losses.

Here's how it works: If you are up the $300—that is, you have a total of $400 in chips in front of you—it means you are winning, and may be on a hot streak. (No time to quit now!)

Put $350 aside—this is money you "lock up"—and continue to play with the other $50. If you lose the $50, walk away with your winnings. You are still up $250.

If you continue to win—say you win another $100, so now you have a total of $500 in chips in front of you—then you now "lock up" $400, and continue to play with the remaining $100.

If you drop back down to the money you have "locked up" *walk away!* (This takes great discipline, but do it.)

If you continue winning beyond this point, consider raising the amount you are betting per hand.

The basic idea of this "up side" strategy is once you have attained your initial goal, continue playing and you could continue winning. As your winnings continue to grow, at some point the tide will change and you will begin to lose. The idea is to quit playing when you have dropped back 10 to 20 percent from the most you were up beyond attaining your initial goal.

## PROGRESSIVE BETTING

Warning, this method is not statistically sound—but even the brightest blackjack players have seen it work and believe it can work. And, since I recognize that not everyone reading this book is going to go to a casino and try to make a living playing blackjack, this method is a lot of fun—IF you're winning. Try this only if you are up and are on a total roll, or if you are feeling wild.

Here is how it works: Each time you win a hand, you add one more chip to the previous bet.

Your first bet is $5 and you win. Now you have $10. Bet it all. If you lose, you are still even. You win again. Now you have $20. Bet $15 of it and put the remaining $5 in your untouchable pile—in other words, lock it up. You win again. If you win again you bet $30 and lock up another $10, to make your total of locked up money $15. If you can keep your streak going to the point where you win a $25 bet, you will have $50 locked away. However, if you lose the last $25 bet you are still up $30, and then you begin again with a five-dollar bet. If you win the last $25 bet, you can rake back $20 of it and add five dollars more to the next bet. Your next bet will be $30. Your total is up to $70, not counting the $30 which is bet on the next hand.

At some point, you have to stop the progression and either start again at five dollars, or if you are up pretty good, start betting $10 or $20 a hand.

If you get up big, start betting big, but keep "locking up" some of it. I'll say it again: Never risk money which you have locked up! If you get down to the money you have "locked up", don't walk away, *run away!*

Remember: 1) bet big with their money when you are up; 2) bet small with your own money when you are even or down.

Of course mathematical probabilities are one thing, and then there is blackjack. Any blackjack player will tell you that there are elements of the game that a slide rule just won't help with. Call it a gambler's superstition, but blackjack is a "streaky" game.

The way it usually goes is: You stay the same, stay the same, lose a little, stay the same, stay the same, lose a little, stay the same, stay the same, lose a little, stay the same, stay the same, lose a little—then you win a lot in a short amount of time, say 10 to 15 minutes. Try to recognize the short winning streaks and press your bets for that short time. This, you will find, is easier said than done.

## SYSTEMS TO AVOID

Anyone who hangs around in a casino long enough will run into the blackjack "expert" who has a system that cannot fail. He will tell you all about it, and—if you don't think it through—the system might sound pretty good.

The system, referred to in some areas as the Small Martingale, goes like this. Each time you lose a hand, you double your bet. After you win you return to your smallest bet. Therefore if you bet one dollar and lose, then bet two dollars and lose and then bet four dollars and win, you're up a buck.

You can't lose, right?

No matter how many hands you lose in a row, you have to win one sooner or later and that means that the worst you can do is be a dollar up. You can't lose—or so your "expert" friend on the next bar stool will tell you.

The trouble with the system is it doesn't work, and there is a simple reason. Every blackjack table has a maximum bet.

Let's say the table at which you're playing has a maximum bet of $500. You lose nine consecutive hands (one dollar, two dollars, four dollars, eight dollars, $16, $32, $64, $128, $256), so what do you do? You are out $511 and your next bet will be $512, right? Win that one and you're a buck up, right? Wrong. The table doesn't allow it. The maximum bet is $500. You are out your $511.

So remember, any system that uses money management alone as the key to its success is bogus. No systematized fluctuation in the sizes of your bets can alter the house's advantage one iota. The only way to do that is to make informed decisions with your cards and that means counting.

## ADJUSTING TO THE RULES

Professional blackjack players are constantly attempting to fine tune their systems to maximize the efficiency of their earning power. To do this, they make slight adjustments to their basic strategy based upon the specific rules of the game they are playing.

For example, there are different plays one would make with a six-deck shoe than with a four-deck shoe, and by this I mean adjustments above and beyond those you make upon the running count to determine the True Count.

Play will be slightly different at a table where doubling down is allowed on any hand and as opposed to those where doubling down is allowed only with a total of nine,10 or 11.

If doubling down after splitting your hand is not allowed, this will affect strategy. The number of times that splitting is allowed during the same round will have an effect, as will whether or not the dealer stands when he holds a soft 17, and whether or not surrendering and early surrendering are allowed.

The specific rules used at various casinos and regions are listed below. Once you know the rules you will be playing under, you can find the appropriate charts to show you the best basic strategy for that set of rules at the back of this book.

# CHAPTER SIX
# CASINO SPECIFICS

Since blackjack—or 21, as it is still known in some places—is a game that is played all around the world, it should come as no shock that the rules are slightly different depending on what country or area you are in.

Heck, in some places the rules of blackjack change from casino to casino—or even from table to table—so it is important that you know what the rules are and gear your strategy to them.

We are going to go spanning the globe now, to the many places of the world where blackjack is popular, looking at the specifications of the game.

## ON THE BOARDWALK

In Atlantic City there are a certain number of blackjack rules that are consistent from casino to casino:

> More than two decks are used in all games.
> All players' cards are dealt face up.
> Dealers must stand on a soft 17.
> Doubling down is allowed after splitting pairs.
> There is no re-splitting of Aces.
> A player may double down on any two cards except those with a point total of 21.

All of the Atlantic City casinos offer an eight-deck shoe, while the Atlantis, Bally's, the Castle, the Claridge, Resorts, the Sans, and the Tropicana also offer a six-deck option.

## IN LAS VEGAS

In some clubs of Las Vegas the standard rules are the same as those in Atlantic City—with the exception of doubling down after splitting pairs, which is allowed in Atlantic City but only in some clubs in Las Vegas. A smaller percentage of Las Vegas tables offer an eight-deck shoe, with the six-deck shoe being the largest at most casinos. This, of course, means that the chances of winning in Vegas are better than in New Jersey, probably because the competition between casinos is hotter, with less cooperation between the casinos. And, unlike in Atlantic City, many Las Vegas casinos still offer one- or two-deck games.

The Bellagio Casino is experimenting with dealing all cards face up at some of its double-deck games. The public reason for this move, one that doesn't quite wash if you think about it, is that a team of card sharks are marking cards.

In a face-up only game, the players never actually touch the cards, therefore it is impossible to mark them. (The reason the excuse doesn't work is that they don't explain why the card markers wouldn't simply move to a table where the face-up only rules were not being used.)

Best bet is that research has shown that, when players are not allowed to touch their cards, more hands per hour can be played, thus increasing the casino's take.

Some casinos, including the Rio in Las Vegas, do not shuffle the cards left in the shoe after all of the players have left the table. When a new player (or players) enters a game, the dealer merely starts dealing from the spot where he left off at the old game, without a fresh shuffle. Card counters, in such a situation, may distinguish themselves to casino surveillance by requesting a fresh shuffle, or not starting play until that shoe is empty.

In order to make their casino more attractive than the extremely similar casino next door (and across the street and down the block), Las Vegas blackjack tables have been experimenting with paying off two-to-one for some combinations that make 21. Some casinos pay twice the normal amount for a hand of Sixes, Sevens, or Eights of the same suit. Some pay double for a hand of three Sevens. In both cases, however, the dealer still wins if he has blackjack and it's still a push if he gets 21.

Some casinos pay off two-to-one when a player gets a blackjack consisting of the Ace and Jack of Spades. If the dealer also has a blackjack, no matter which two cards form it, the hand is a push.

You can receive two-to-one in some places by taking three hits before accumulating 21 points. A five-card 21 doesn't happen very often and the player who goes for it has a lot of courage. Again, if the dealer has 21 it is a push. If the dealer has blackjack, you lose, even if you have ten Twos and an Ace.

Caesars Palace in Las Vegas offers four varieties of blackjack. They have single- and double-deck games, both of which are dealt by hand; "multiple" deck 21 dealt from a shoe and Over/Under 13, a new sidebet in which you bet your first two cards will total over or under 13. When playing Over/Under 13, Aces always count as one and you lose if your total is exactly 13.

## ELSEWHERE IN NEVADA

In Reno and Lake Tahoe, Nevada, the standard rules are the same as those in Las Vegas, except you may only double down when holding a two-card hand with a total point value of 10 or 11.

## CONNECTICUT

One casino with a reputation for being lenient toward card counters is Foxwoods in Connecticut—although that may no longer be true after they read this. Foxwoods is like the friendly cop on the beat who lets the teenagers drink behind the theater as long as they hide it when he walks by. The first teenager who shows that cop up by drinking in his face gets busted. At Foxwoods counters are tolerated unless they try to make a living at it, betting heavily on a regular schedule or over long stretches.

Foxwoods' primary competitor, the Mohegan Sun, on a nearby Indian reservation also in Connecticut, used computer software (called "Safe Jack") to track card counters, and it has been known to expel counters who bet large amounts of money.

## MINNESOTA

The best place to play blackjack in Minnesota is the Jackpot Junction Casino Hotel on the land of the Lower Sioux Indian Community in the town of Morton. The Jackpot has 44 blackjack tables which operate on Las Vegas rules. Players can split pairs up to four hands (excluding Aces), and play any two positions at one time. Betting limits vary from $2 to $500. The real reason to go to Jackpot, however, are the number of two-deck games being played, more than in any other casino in the region.

## INTERNATIONAL RULES

For those globetrotters interested in playing blackjack outside the continental United States, here's an idea of what rule peculiarities you might expect to find.

In PUERTO RICO, there is no re-splitting of pairs, although you may double down after splitting. There is no restriction on which cards you may double down on, and, if the dealer has blackjack, you lose only your original bet while getting to keep your doubled-down bet.

In the NETHERLANDS, it is okay to re-split pairs. You may double down only when you have a two-card total of nine, 10 or 11. If the dealer has blackjack, you lose all of your split and doubled-down bets.

North of the border, in CANADA, doubling down is restricted to those with two-card totals of 10 or 11 and doubling down after splitting a pair is prohibited.

In GERMANY, there is no re-splitting pairs. Here's a peculiar rule, which is also in effect in Belgium and Austria: a doubled-down Ace-Eight hand, when a Two is drawn, is worth only 11. Doubling down is only allowed when you hold a two-card total of nine, 10 or 11. There is no hole card, and the entire doubled-down and split bets are lost if the dealer has blackjack.

The rules in AUSTRIA are the same as those in Germany.

In FRANCE, there is no hole card and doubling down is allowed after splitting pairs. Doubling down is allowed only for players with two-card totals of nine, 10 or 11.

In the UNITED KINGDOM, the rules favor the house more so than in the rest of the world. Players may buy insurance only when they have a blackjack. There is no re-splitting of pairs. You may not split pairs of Fours, Fives, or Sixes. You may only double down if you have a two-card total of nine, 10 or 11. Entire doubled-down and split bets are lost if the dealer has blackjack.

That's the bad news. The good news is that, in Great Britain, there is none of the player versus casino feel that you find in the rest of the world. Because of their confidence that they will win anyway—due to the size of the house advantage—casinos even display a simple version of basic strategy at every table, and they have been known to give advice to players who become confused. And not lousy advice, like a desperate pit boss on the Vegas strip might give, but helpful, the real goods. Also, if you are going to be gambling in Great Britain, be aware that to do it legally, you must have a license, and that the license must be in effect for forty-eight hours before you can play. This doesn't necessarily mean that you have to lengthen your vacation. It may be possible to successfully apply for a gambling license by mail so that you are legal and ready to go as soon as you get there.

In BELGIUM, along with the Ace-Eight being worth only 11 when a Two is drawn, all doubled-down and split bets are lost when the dealer has blackjack. Doubling down is allowed only when you have a two-card total of nine, 10 or 11.

In AUSTRALIA, no re-splitting of pairs is allowed, doubling down is restricted to totals of nine, 10 and 11, and all doubled-down and split bets are lost if the dealer has blackjack.

# BLACKJACK TOURNAMENTS

Some casinos offer blackjack tournaments in which players who fancy themselves as skilled play with tournament chips instead of casino chips. After paying an entrance fee, all players start with the same number of chips.

When the tourney is complete, the chips are counted and the player who has the most chips wins. The winning prize is usually somewhere in the neighborhood of half the entire purse.

The Jackpot Junction Casino Hotel in Morton, Minnesota, holds a regular blackjack tournament that has first-round play on Saturday, a last-chance first round on Sunday morning, and the semi-finals and the finals on Sunday evening.

Their purses have been as high as $50,000 per tournament with the winner getting $25,000. Here are their tournament rules, which are pretty representative of how these things are run:

1) Five dollar minimum bet.
2) $100 maximum bet.
3) Each round will consist of 30 hands.
4) After a bet has been made, it cannot be changed.
5) Each player is allowed only one spot at the table.
6) Doubling down is allowed.
7) All tournament chips must be kept separated by denomination and in full view of all players.
8) Coaching is NOT allowed.
9) In the event of a tie, additional hands will be dealt until the tie is broken. In the final round, only a tie for first place will be broken.
10) Calculators, pens and paper are NOT allowed.

# CHAPTER SEVEN
# REASONS TO BEWARE

## CASINO SURVEILLANCE

You can tell that you are getting to be a good blackjack player not just when you go home with more money than you started with, but when casinos begin to keep an eye on you.

(You know you've become very, very good when they ask you to leave. At that point it is time to get clever.)

That doesn't mean you are cheating or doing something illegal. It merely means that they don't like what you are doing, and they are going to do their best to keep you from doing it.

When card counting became popular, casinos became very afraid (panicky might be a better word) about losing all of their money at their suddenly beatable blackjack tables. All of a sudden, all dealers were dealing out of shoes, which held far more decks than could be shuffled by hand. And, worse than that, card counters who were still successful were hassled by management.

Asked to leave.

Even today, all casinos keep a team of employees whose job it is to keep track of (and get rid of) blackjack players who repeatedly win more than they lose. Over the years the techniques used by these spies have become increasingly sophisticated.

For example, the Atlantis Casino in Nassau, Bahamas, now uses computer tracking software designed to analyze each player's betting, and to determine whether or not that player is using a card-counting or shuffle-tracking system.

That same software is also used at the Mohegan Sun casino, in Connecticut, and at the Resorts International, in Atlantic City, New Jersey. The three casinos using the system share common ownership.

Since professional blackjack players have caught on that they are being watched and scrutinized as they play, they have learned to never stay in one place for very long.

They move from dealer to dealer, and from casino to casino, in hopes of making as much money as possible before the casino surveillance catches up to what they are doing.

The conspiracy to keep the casinos, rather than the players, in the dough is huge. The casinos even maintain communication systems between each other to track professional players.

Casinos have the right to ban anyone from playing any game at any time for any reason—so if it looks to them as if you have "beaten the system" they won't hesitate to give you the boot.

Professional gamblers (or those who for whatever reason consider themselves professional gamblers) have often tried to find a blackjack table that is in a corner or in dim light, in hopes that surveillance cameras would be less apt to see them. At this point, such a move is meaningless. About all it will get the gambler is eye strain.

The surveillance cameras used in modern casinos are so sophisticated that they do not need a heck of a lot of light to produce an identifiable image of the gambler.

The system currently used in large casinos is called the "Subtle Casino Lighting and Surveillance." The cameras,

## BEWARE OVERZEALOUS CASINO SECURITY

Two brothers, Frederick and Steven Barthelme, were arrested several years ago and charged with attempting to fix a blackjack game, a crime that is punishable by up to two years in prison.

The charges stemmed from a surveillance tape which, according to the Grand Casino in Gulfport, Mississippi, showed the dealer giving the brothers signals to tell them when to take out insurance.

After two years of being threatened with prison, the charges were eventually dismissed by a Mississippi State Circuit judge after an expert from Las Vegas examined the surveillance tapes and found that the dealer's "signals" were merely habits that she had, and that they stemmed from boredom, and the repetitiveness of her job.

The case earned notoriety because the Barthelme brothers are writers who have written about their devastating gambling addiction—one that has cost them hundreds of thousands of dollars at the blackjack tables.

It seems to me that a couple of regular customers like that would have been treated more politely by the Grand Casino, but I wasn't there, and there are always intangibles.

usually mounted on the ceiling, are no larger than a lady's lipstick and work in any light.

## CARD COUNTING IS NOT ILLEGAL

The Nevada casinos did, at one point, try to get card counters arrested for cheating, but a Nevada judge determined that card counters were simply using a greater level of skill than the typical blackjack player.

Blackjack players, the judge said, are free to use any information that is made available to them, provided that there is no collusion between a player and casino personnel.

Although there is no law in Nevada, or anywhere else, against counting cards when playing blackjack at a casino, the casinos do have the law on their side when it comes to preventing card counters from playing at their tables.

If a card counter persists in attempting to play at a casino that does not want them, the casino can call in the local law enforcement and have the dirty card counter arrested for trespassing.

## YOU BETTER SHOP AROUND . . .

One way in which to play a lot of blackjack without making the casino suspicious that you are counting cards is to break up your playing. Do not spend many hours every day with the same dealer at the same table.

Move around. Play at one table for an hour, then move someplace else. Play some in the morning, some in the afternoon and some at night. This way you will be appearing for a short period of time in front of three different shifts of employees (spies).

# INTERNET BLACKJACK

Before partaking of an internet casino, there are a few things you'll want to determine. (Actually, many of these tips are true of any web site that requires your credit card number.)

How attractive is the site? A fly-by-night operation will often have a fly-by-night look. Are there warnings and assurances regarding the confidentiality of the information they are requesting from you? There should be.

Is it easy to contact the proprietor of the site? Is there a phone number? An address to write to—one that isn't just a post office box? Are they e-mail accessible? If so, write them a note and see how quickly they answer. In other words, make sure someone is home.

If you plan to put any money at all into on-line gambling, and you have the slightest doubt about the site at which you are playing, call the Better Business Bureau and make sure everything is on the up and up.

There are internet sites that allow you to play blackjack without wagering—although you will inevitably be pestered by on-screen invitations to gamble. These sites are excellent for practicing your basic strategy. However, card-counting is a skill that must be practiced in a casino, or at home with a set-up that simulates a casino.

# CHAPTER EIGHT
## INTERVIEW
## WITH A PRO

We dug out a professional blackjack player on the East Coast who we will refer to as Eric Ketchem. (He doesn't want to be known by his real name for fear that his "favorite" pit bosses might be reading this.)

Here is a portion of our Q&A session:

Q: Where is your favorite place to play blackjack?

A: By far my favorite place to play is Las Vegas, but not every club in Las Vegas. The reasons for this are: first, Las Vegas has a greater availability of single- and double-deck games. As a counter, my advantage decreases tremendously when six- to eight-deck shoes are being used. In addition, even without counting, and using only basic strategy, statistically, the fewer the decks, the less the odds against you are. That's partially because, in a single-deck game, the dealer cannot get Two, Two, Two, Two, Two, Two, Two, Seven.

Another reason is less-than-crowded tables. Statistically, the fewer people playing at the table, the better the odds are for the player (head to head being optimal). One reason for this is, if I'm playing head to head, the dealer and I will get blackjack the same number of times. He gets four and I get four. I lose my bet four times, *but* I win one-and-a-half times my bet four times for a net gain of two bets. If there are four other players and me and the dealer, the dealer and I will still get an equal number of blackjacks. We will each get 1/6th of the blackjacks dealt at the table, six hands per round. So, I am better off with the dealer and I each getting six blackjacks per shoe—so that I am the equivalent of three bets up—than with the dealer and I each getting one blackjack per shoe, for a net gain of only one-half bet. Also, when playing head to head, when the deck becomes a favorable count, it will stay favorable longer—that is, for more rounds of play, because many fewer cards are being dealt per round.

Also: a few clubs in Vegas, mostly downtown, offer some really good rules. There are places that allow doubling down on any Two, Three, or Four cards. They don't advertise it but they allow it. Blackjack conditions in Vegas can be found on the internet where the rules for each blackjack game—unlike Atlantic City—vary for each club. Some allow doubling down after split, others don't. At some places, the dealer hits on soft 17. At others, he doesn't. Some only allow doubling down on Nine, Ten, or Eleven. It is important to use a basic strategy that is tailored to the rules of the particular game that you are playing—for example, the number of decks being used, whether or not the dealer hits a soft 17, whether doubling down after splitting is allowed, whether surrendering is available, and so on.

In Atlantic City, things are simpler. The blackjack rules are governed by the New Jersey Gaming Commission, and, therefore, all the rules for all the clubs in Atlantic City are basically the same, although I don't think the commission prohibits giving the player better odds than their guidelines.

My personal favorite places to play in Las Vegas currently are: The Mirage, which has good rules and offers a double-deck game; Treasure Island; Circus Circus; and Binions Horseshoe, which offers a $25 single-deck game.

Note the rules for each club change often. And the last reason I like Vegas is that it is an unbelievable town! Disneyland for gamblers! Sin City! I hear there is a lot of family stuff there, too. The food is the best anywhere (the buffet at the Flamingo is great, although their blackjack game is so-so) and comps for free food, rooms, and cigarettes are plentiful for moderate players.

Q: Have you had any dealings with casino security because you are a card counter?

A: No, I've never been banned or anything.

Q: How do you avoid it?

A: Well, I'm a small player betting $25 to $100 per hand. Only on very rare occasions—when I am up big—do I bet up to $150. Remember though, if you got $100 up and then split out three hands, and then double down on two of them, that's $500 out on the table!

Q: Any heat from the casinos at all?

A: Heat is another thing altogether. I have received heat at various times, and it takes on many forms. I don't believe I have received heat necessarily because they thought I was counting, only because I was winning. I have had pit critters (pit bosses) hang over me and silently watch my play intently. To this I usually say something like, "I can't believe how lucky I am today! I've almost gotten back to even on all the money I lost this morning at that other blankety-blank casino." Remember, they know how much you've won or lost in their casino. Other times (this is more often the case) the pit bosses or pit supervisor will come over and try to start up a conversation while I am playing. It's amazing how this only happens when I am winning. "Where you from?" "What do you do?" When this happens I only respond with brief answers and try not to encourage any further conversation. If they persist to the point where I am losing my count, I cash in and leave—or go to another pit or another club. They won this round.

Another thing that happens, which is a form of heat, is this: Normally one dealer deals at a particular table for 40 minutes, and the relief dealer comes in for 20 minutes, then the main dealer comes back. On occasion—this also only seems to happen while winning—the house will switch in another dealer, usually a really, really fast dealer—but sometimes a very slow one. Logically, one would think this shouldn't matter, the cards don't know who is dealing them, but somehow it seems to end a winning streak. I've had it happen many times.

They may go so far as to have the big breasted waitress come over and flirt with you, or empty the ashtrays. This seems like a little thing, but the pit critters are as superstitious as the gamblers, and they will make a small change like the ashtrays just to try to "break the streak." I myself have been known to always pee in the same urinal, or not tie my untied shoes while on a streak. I know this is silly, but why tempt fate? Another thing that happens is the pit critter will come and raise the minimum bet for that table. Raising the minimum bet during disadvantageous counts severely decreases one's advantage. The only way to counter the effect is to increase your maximum bet. If I am playing a $25 to $100 spread, and they raise the minimum to $50, I now must play a $50 to $200 spread to compensate. Usually the sign on the table says the house can change the stakes on one-half-hour notice. On one occasion, in a club in Atlantic City, every time I went to a table, they came by and raised the limit. I would go to another table and then the same thing would happen there, and it kept happening! The next time I played in that club (at least a month later), I said, "Screw the comps, I'm not giving them my comp card cause I don't want them to know who I am." I was registered in a room at that hotel, and to my surprise, after playing for maybe one hour, a pit boss came up to me and said, "Hello, Mr. Ketchem, how come you haven't given us your card? Don't you want to be rated?" I said, "How did you know who I am?" and he said that he remembered me from last time. I doubt that this guy remembers the thousands of people who play each month, I suspect that they have my picture on file, and a computer that can call it up when compared to a live picture, but perhaps I'm just paranoid. At any rate, that incident really surprised me.

Q: Tell us about some of the funny things that have happened to you at the blackjack table.

A: My wife and I were playing at the same table. I was at Third Base and she was at First—that is, the last and first spots at the table. An obnoxious drunk sat down in the middle spot. Shortly after that my wife got up and declared something like "I'm going to go play where there aren't any obnoxious drunks!" After this, the guy turns to me and says "Boy, I pity the guy who's married to that bitch!" I looked at him calmly and said, "I am." He then sheepishly said he was going to play at another table.

On one utterly disastrous trip to Atlantic City—I had lost my limit and was waiting for the people I went there with to be ready to go home—I was playing minimum bets at a five-dollar table, just biding my time. I was still counting the cards, and, in an exceptionally good count, I let my bet ride for six consecutive winning hands. In those six hands my five dollars turned into $320! I would never ordinarily do this, but I was already tapped and figured if I lost any one of the bets along the way I was only out the original five dollars and no worse off than I started. I pulled back the $320, and I don't remember if I won the next hand after that. My friends came and got me, but I was still down pretty big.

The first time I ever played in Atlantic City, maybe the third or fourth time I ever played, before I knew much about blackjack—I knew some of the basic strategy—I won a bundle, for me. My entire strategy at a five-dollar table was when I was up $100 I bet $10 per hand, when I was up $300 I bet $30 per hand, when I was up $500 I bet $50 per hand, when I was up $1000 I bet $100 per hand, till the point where I was up over $3,000—although I never really went to betting $300 per hand.

I remember the pit people whispering to each other and pointing in my direction. At the time, I really didn't know how miraculous this was. I gave some of it back, but ended leaving town up $1,800. Not bad. There is something to be said for beginner's luck. Something you invariably hear people say at the table is, "I'd rather be lucky than good." I'd rather be both.

Q: What advice would you have for people who are intimidated at the thought of counting cards?

A: My counting skills are something that have evolved. Counting itself is really not that hard. It's funny, I can count an eight-deck shoe, but when my hand or the dealer's hand grows to be about five or six cards in size because of taking hits and getting small cards, I can't add them up very fast at all.

I've even been known to ask the dealer, "What do I have?" (Saying things like that is not a bad idea even if you can count lickety-split. Do anything you can to convince the dealer—or any employee of the casino, for that matter—that you aren't the brightest bulb in the box.)

Anyway, my point is that you don't have to have the world's greatest arithmetic skills to count cards. It's a matter of practice.

To those who are intimidated, I would say, first of all, one does not "count" every card in the shoe. I always sit at Third Base. The initial cards are dealt, two to each player and one up card to the dealer.

In almost all shoe games all of the player's cards are dealt face up. All the players' hands are initially in pairs. If one player has a Queen and a King, while another has a Three and a Six, the two high cards cancel out the two low ones, so all four cards are ignored—as are the Sevens, Eights, and Nines.

In addition, any hand initially dealt that has one high card and one low card, such as a King and a Six, is also ignored since plus one added to minus one equals zero.

When the cards are dealt, I scan the table from First Base across to Third Base. I finish my count by counting my own cards. I cancel out what I can and count the rest. Only then do I add the dealer's up card to the count.

Then, when the dealer starts asking the players if they want a hit, starting with First Base, I count all of the hit cards as they are dealt out. By the time it is time for me to play my hand, I am all "caught up" and only have to add my own hit cards to the count.

After that the dealer plays his hand, and it stays there for a moment while the dealer pays off or collects bets. When looking at the dealer's played-out hand, the second card from the right is the dealer's original up card—the one I have already counted. So I ignore it and add in, or cancel out, the other dealer cards.

One word of caution: while scanning the initially dealt cards, try to be aware of what the first and second player's hit cards are as they receive them. If they bust, those cards are going to be immediately scooped away into the discard pile, so you won't get a second chance to count them.

It does take practice, at home and in casino conditions, but once learned it becomes automatic. I can count cards, order a drink from the waitress (soda only, no alcohol, save that for later) and talk to the other players all at the same time.

As to fears of it all going too fast, you have got nothing to lose, even if you don't catch all the cards at first, some idea of the composition of the deck is better than none at all.

When playing blackjack, the player never (in the long run) wins more than 50 percent of the hands. You always lose more hands than you win. That's a fact.

The only way to win money is to lose your small bets and win your big bets, and to make big bets when the remaining cards in the deck are in your favor, and small bets when they are not.

If you play blackjack and flat bet (bet the same amount every hand) you will not win in the long run. Start off counting the cards, as best as you can, and altering the size of your bet according to the count (bigger bets in plus two counts or better, minimum bets in counts less than that).

# GLOSSARY

**Act**—Personality and/or disguise assumed by a card counter to keep from being identified.

**Action**—Total amount of money bet.

**Advantage per Total Bets**—percentage obtained by dividing the total amount won by the total amount bet on all hands, including doubles, splits and insurance wagers.

**Back Counting**—Standing behind players and counting cards, then entering the game only when the ratios are in the players' favor. Also known as Wonging, after Stanford Wong, the pseudonym of a noted blackjack writer.

**Balanced Count**—A card-counting system that starts at zero, then adds and subtracts as appropriate for the types of cards that have been seen. Such a system would end at zero as well if all cards were seen.

**Basic Strategy**—A strategy of play designed to minimize the house advantage without the use of card counting. Most card counting systems are based on the basic truths of the basic strategy, however.

**Bet Sizing**—Increasing or decreasing the sizes of your bets depending on whether the True Count is positive or negative.

**Bet Spread**—The ratio between the smallest and largest bets placed by a player during one shoe. If a player's early bets are $10, and he increases to $100 when he feels the odds are more in his favor, then he is said to be using a 10–1 bet spread.

**Blackjack**—The best hand you can have. An Ace combined with a face card or a Ten.

**Burn Card(s)**—Before a dealer deals from a fresh deck or shoe, he shuffles the cards and the cards are cut by one of the players. At that point, the dealer discards one or more cards, which are not dealt to the players from that deck or shoe.

**Bust**—After taking a hit, a losing accumulation of points greater than 21 is a bust.

**Card counting**—Any of several playing strategies whereby the player keeps a running count of which cards have already been played and which remain in the deck or shoe, thus knowing when his chances of beating the dealer are maximized. Players bet low when the odds are against them and high when the odds are in their favor. Card counting has been banned by casinos, so players who are caught are usually asked to leave.

**Card Weight**—Assigned value to a type of card by a card counter to make it easy to count, usually +1 or −1.

**Count**—The running number in a card counter's head that tells him the ratio of low cards to high cards remaining in the shoe, and, therefore, how much he should bet on a given hand. A.k.a. running count.

**Cover Bet**—A move of subterfuge. This is a bet placed by a card counting player that is inappropriate to his system (usually a large bet early in a shoe) to throw off the dealer or casino personnel who might suspect him as a card counter.

**Cut Card**—A colored plastic card used to cut the cards after they have been shuffled by the dealer.

**Cutoff**—Point in the shoe at which the remaining cards remain unplayed, all of the cards are shuffled together, and the dealer starts over. The cutoff point is usually determined by the placement of the cut card.

**Dealer**—The person who represents the house, deals the cards, determines the outcome of the game, and settles wagers.

**Deck Penetration**—See Penetration.

**Double Down**—Casino rule that allows a player to increase his bet, up to double, on any hand other than blackjack. The choice to double down must be made when the player has only two cards. After doubling down, the player is allowed to take only one additional card.

**Doubling for Less**—Increasing your bet after receiving two cards but by less than double, which is the maximum.

**Down card**—Any face down card, also known as the hole card.

**Draw**—Take another card. Take a hit.

**Early Surrender**—Surrender that is allowed by the dealer even though the dealer has a natural blackjack. Most casinos do not allow early surrender.

**Efficiency**—Ratio between the actual gain in winnings achieved through counting cards and the possible gain in winnings. Betting efficiency is the percentage of cases in which a particular counting system predicts when a bet should be raised. Playing efficiency refers to the percentage of time that a counting system predicts, correctly, when play should vary from the basic strategy.

**Even Money**—If you take insurance while holding blackjack, betting that the dealer has blackjack also, you win the amount of your bet, rather than a three-to-two payoff, whether or not the dealer has blackjack.

**Eye in the Sky**—Surveillance cameras placed above blackjack tables that allow house security to follow play and watch the players.

**First Base**—When facing the dealer, the seat on the far right. The player who sits there is called the First Baseman and receives his cards first.

**Flat Bettor**—A player who bets the same amount on each round.

**Floor man**—Person responsible for overseeing a group of several blackjack tables, usually the dealers' immediate supervisor.

**Hard**—As in "Hard 15." All hands that contain no Ace are considered hard, as well as those that do contain an Ace when that Ace is counted as having a value of one.

**Head On, or Heads Up**—Playing one-on-one with the dealer; playing at a table where you are the only player.

**Hit Me**—To ask the dealer for another card.

**Hole Card**—A card that is face down.

**Insurance**—A side bet whereby the player bets that the dealer has blackjack. The player is allowed to bet up to half of his original bet. If the dealer has blackjack, the insurance bet pays two-to-one.

**Insurance correlation**—Relationship between the card weights as counted by a player and his winning insurance bets. A positive correlation would mean that the player's card counting has enhanced his ability to predict when the dealer has blackjack.

**London Deal**—Deal in which two cards are delivered face up to the players, while the dealer gives himself only one card, also face up. The dealer does not give himself a second card until all of the players have completed their play.

**Mechanic**—A cheater who manipulates cards.

**Minus Count**—A running count or True Count that is below zero, indicating that there are a disproportionately large number of low cards remaining in the shoe—and that conditions are not favorable to the player. Some players will not play when there is a minus count. They play only when there is a better than average chance of winning.

**Natural**—A two-card hand that equals 21 without taking a hit.

**Nevada Deal**—Deal in which the cards are delivered face down to the players, while the dealer deals himself one card face down and another face up.

**Over/Under**—A brand new twist to the game, but still unavailable at most casinos, whereby a player can place a side bet that the first two players' cards will either add up to over 13 or under 13.

**Pack**—The set of cards in play. A game that uses an eight-deck shoe is using a 416-card pack.

**Pat**—A hand that totals 17, 18, 19, 20, or 21.

**Penetration**—The percentage of cards that have been dealt out of a shoe before the dealer reshuffles. If the dealer gets three-quarters, or 75 percent of the way through the shoe before reshuffling he is said to have given the players "good penetration."

**Pinch**—Method of cheating whereby a player attempts to remove chips from his bet after seeing his cards. This technique is not recommended for those who enjoy life.

**Pit**—Arrangement of blackjack tables in a semi-circle so that players stay on the outside and casino personnel stay on the inside.

**Pit Boss**—The person in charge of the pit, usually the immediate supervisor of the floor men.

**Plus Count**—Card count in which your running count is in the positive numbers, indicating that there is a greater than normal percentage of high cards remaining in the shoe.

**Preferential Shuffling**—Dealers who aid the cause of the house by shuffling when the cards are in the players' favor and not shuffling when they are in the house's favor.

**Press**—Method of cheating whereby you ever-so-discreetly add chips to your bet after you have seen your cards. Players who attempt this often run out of luck quickly.

**Push**—A tie. You and the dealer end up with the same hand, so no money exchanges hands. (The only time a push could result in the exchanging of money would be on the rare occasion when a player took out insurance while holding blackjack, and the dealer had blackjack also.)

**Round**—Dealer and the players play one hand.

**Running Count**—The ever-changing number a card counter keeps in his head, which is based on the values of all exposed cards since the dealer last shuffled.

**Shill**—A casino employee who will pretend to be a player and put on an act designed to get other people to play there.

**Shoe**—A box, usually made out of plastic, that holds multiple decks of cards, more decks than could be dealt with a dealer's hands alone. The shoe was necessitated by card counters.

**Shuffle Tracking**—A system, mystical to most, whereby the player determines which sections of the deck will be favorable by memorizing the cards' position before the shuffle and watching the shuffle carefully.

**Side Count**—Any count kept in the player's head that is additional to and separate from the running count. The most common side count is of Aces exposed since the last shuffle.

**Soft**—As in "Soft 17." A hand that includes an Ace in which that Ace is being counted as having a value of 11. A soft 17 can also be worth seven if you choose to count the Ace as one instead of 11. Players will take a hit more boldly with a soft hand for this reason.

**Split**—If a player's first two cards match (i.e. two Sevens), this casino rule allows a player to split those cards and play two hands, thus doubling his bet on the round. The player must bet the same amount on the second hand as he did on the first. Most casinos allow a player to split up to four times per round. (Players are, in most houses, also allowed to double down after splitting. But, again, the rules state that the player must bet the same amount on each new hand as he did on his original hand.) If the cards that are being split happen to be Aces, the player is allowed to add only one card to each hand. One negative to doubling down is that, if a card worth ten points is drawn to join one or both of the Aces, those hands are not blackjack—although they are worth 21 points. Therefore, if the dealer has blackjack, he beats an Ace-Ten combination from a player who has doubled down.

**Spread**—The ratio of your largest bet to your smallest bet.

**Stand**—To stick with the number of cards you already have; to stand pat.

**Stiff Hand**—A loser. A hand that has a poor chance of winning, regardless of strategy. A hard total of 12 through 16 fits the bill.

**Strategy Variations**—These are instances when a player will bet or play in contrast to the basic strategy of blackjack, based on his card count.

**Surrender**—If your situation is so bleak (say you have two cards totaling 16 and the dealer has a Ten showing) that you feel hopeless, you can surrender right then and there, losing only half of your bet.

**Ten Cards**—Describes all cards worth 10 points: the Tens, Jacks, Queens, Kings, and sometimes the Aces.

**Ten Poor**—Section of the deck with a disproportionately low number of 10 cards.

**Ten Rich**—Portion of the deck that has a disproportionately high number of 10 cards.

**Third Base**—When facing the dealer, the seat at the far left. The player who sits there is called the Third Baseman and receives his cards last.

**Toke**—A tip for the dealer.

**True Count**—The running count divided by the number of unplayed decks in the shoe.

**Unbalanced Count**—Any running count that does not start at zero when the deck is freshly shuffled. Some players start their count at seven, thus reducing the time they will be counting among negative numbers and starting on a number perceived by some as lucky. Other players use an unbalanced system so that they do not have to adjust for a True Count.

**Up Card**—Card received from dealer that is face up.

**Wonging**—Playing when the count is favorable and not playing when it is unfavorable. Derives from "blackjack expert" Stanford Wong. Also known as back-counting. Be aware that two Wongs do not make a Wight.

# BASIC STRATEGY CHARTS

## KEY

A=Ace

dd=double down

sp=split

st=stand

sur=surrender (if surrender is not allowed, take a hit)

sur&=surrender (if surrender is not allowed, split)

## CHART 1

Eight decks

Dealer hits soft 17

Double down on any hand

No doubling down after splitting

| **Hard count** | | | | | **Dealer's Up Card** | | | | | |
|---|---|---|---|---|---|---|---|---|---|---|
| Your hand | 2 | 3 | 4 | 5 | 6 | 7 | 8 | 9 | 10 | A |
| 5 | hit | hit | hit | hit | hit | hit | hit | hit | hit | hit |
| 6 | hit | hit | hit | hit | hit | hit | hit | hit | hit | hit |
| 7 | hit | hit | hit | hit | hit | hit | hit | hit | hit | hit |
| 8 | hit | hit | hit | hit | hit | hit | hit | hit | hit | hit |
| 9 | hit | dd | dd | dd | dd | hit | hit | hit | hit | hit |
| 10 | dd | dd | dd | dd | dd | dd | dd | dd | hit | hit |
| 11 | dd | dd | dd | dd | dd | dd | dd | dd | dd | dd |
| 12 | hit | hit | st | st | st | hit | hit | hit | hit | hit |
| 13 | st | st | st | st | st | hit | hit | hit | hit | sur |
| 14 | st | st | st | st | st | hit | hit | hit | sur | sur |
| 15 | st | st | st | st | st | hit | hit | hit | sur | sur |
| 16 | st | st | st | st | st | hit | hit | sur | sur | sur |
| 17–21 | st | st | st | st | st | st | st | st | st | st |

| **Soft count** | | | | | **Dealer's Up Card** | | | | | |
|---|---|---|---|---|---|---|---|---|---|---|
| Your Hand | 2 | 3 | 4 | 5 | 6 | 7 | 8 | 9 | 10 | A |
| soft 13 | hit | hit | hit | dd | dd | hit | hit | hit | hit | hit |
| soft 14 | hit | hit | hit | dd | dd | hit | hit | hit | hit | hit |
| soft 15 | hit | hit | dd | dd | dd | hit | hit | hit | hit | hit |
| soft 16 | hit | hit | dd | dd | dd | hit | hit | hit | hit | hit |
| soft 17 | hit | dd | dd | dd | dd | hit | hit | hit | hit | hit |
| soft 18 | dd | dd | dd | dd | dd | st | st | hit | hit | hit |
| soft 19,20 | st | st | st | st | st | st | st | st | st | st |

| **Pairs** | | | | | **Dealer's Up Card** | | | | | |
|---|---|---|---|---|---|---|---|---|---|---|
| Your Hand | 2 | 3 | 4 | 5 | 6 | 7 | 8 | 9 | 10 | A |
| 2,2 | hit | hit | sp | sp | sp | sp | hit | hit | hit | hit |
| 3,3 | hit | hit | sp | sp | sp | sp | hit | hit | hit | hit |
| 4,4 | hit | hit | hit | hit | hit | hit | hit | hit | hit | hit |
| 5,5 | dd | dd | dd | dd | dd | dd | dd | dd | hit | hit |

| | 2 | 3 | 4 | 5 | 6 | 7 | 8 | 9 | 10 | A |
|---|---|---|---|---|---|---|---|---|---|---|
| 6,6 | hit | sp | sp | sp | sp | hit | hit | hit | hit | hit |
| 7,7 | sp | sp | sp | sp | sp | sp | hit | hit | sur | sur |
| 8,8 | sp | sp | sp | sp | sp | sp | sp | sp | sur& | sur& |
| 9,9 | sp | sp | sp | sp | sp | st | sp | sp | st | st |
| 10,10 | st | st | st | st | st | st | st | st | st | st |
| A,A | sp | sp | sp | sp | sp | sp | sp | sp | sp | sp |

## CHART 2

Eight decks

Dealer hits soft 17

Double down on any hand

Doubling down after splitting is allowed

| **Hard count** | **Dealer's Up Card** | | | | | | | | | |
|---|---|---|---|---|---|---|---|---|---|---|
| Your hand | 2 | 3 | 4 | 5 | 6 | 7 | 8 | 9 | 10 | A |
| 5 | hit | hit | hit | hit | hit | hit | hit | hit | hit | hit |
| 6 | hit | hit | hit | hit | hit | hit | hit | hit | hit | hit |
| 7 | hit | hit | hit | hit | hit | hit | hit | hit | hit | hit |
| 8 | hit | hit | hit | hit | hit | hit | hit | hit | hit | hit |
| 9 | hit | dd | dd | dd | dd | hit | hit | hit | hit | hit |
| 10 | dd | dd | dd | dd | dd | dd | dd | dd | hit | hit |
| 11 | dd | dd | dd | dd | dd | dd | dd | dd | dd | dd |
| 12 | hit | hit | st | st | st | hit | hit | hit | hit | hit |
| 13 | st | st | st | st | st | hit | hit | hit | hit | sur |
| 14 | st | st | st | st | st | hit | hit | hit | sur | sur |
| 15 | st | st | st | st | st | hit | hit | hit | sur | sur |
| 16 | st | st | st | st | st | hit | hit | sur | sur | sur |
| 17–21 | st | st | st | st | st | st | st | st | st | st |

| **Soft Count** | **Dealer's Up Card** | | | | | | | | | |
|---|---|---|---|---|---|---|---|---|---|---|
| Your Hand | 2 | 3 | 4 | 5 | 6 | 7 | 8 | 9 | 10 | A |
| soft 13 | hit | hit | hit | dd | dd | hit | hit | hit | hit | hit |

| | | | | | | | | | | |
|---|---|---|---|---|---|---|---|---|---|---|
| soft 14 | hit | hit | hit | dd | dd | hit | hit | hit | hit | hit |
| soft 15 | hit | hit | dd | dd | dd | hit | hit | hit | hit | hit |
| soft 16 | hit | hit | dd | dd | dd | hit | hit | hit | hit | hit |
| soft 17 | hit | dd | dd | dd | dd | hit | hit | hit | hit | hit |
| soft 18 | dd | dd | dd | dd | dd | st | st | hit | hit | hit |
| soft 19,20 | st | st | st | st | st | st | st | st | st | st |

| Pairs | Dealer's Up Card | | | | | | | | | |
|---|---|---|---|---|---|---|---|---|---|---|
| Your Hand | 2 | 3 | 4 | 5 | 6 | 7 | 8 | 9 | 10 | A |
| 2,2 | sp | sp | sp | sp | sp | sp | hit | hit | hit | hit |
| 3,3 | sp | sp | sp | sp | sp | sp | hit | hit | hit | hit |
| 4,4 | hit | hit | hit | sp | sp | hit | hit | hit | hit | hit |
| 5,5 | dd | dd | dd | dd | dd | dd | dd | dd | hit | hit |
| 6,6 | sp | sp | sp | sp | sp | hit | hit | hit | hit | hit |
| 7,7 | sp | sp | sp | sp | sp | sp | hit | hit | sur | sur |
| 8,8 | sp | sp | sp | sp | sp | sp | sp | sp | sur& | sur& |
| 9,9 | sp | sp | sp | sp | sp | st | sp | sp | st | st |
| 10,10 | st | st | st | st | st | st | st | st | st | st |
| A,A | sp | sp | sp | sp | sp | sp | sp | sp | sp | sp |

## CHART 3

Eight decks

Dealer hits soft 17

Double down on any hand

No doubling down after splitting

| Hard count | Dealer's Up Card | | | | | | | | | |
|---|---|---|---|---|---|---|---|---|---|---|
| Your hand | 2 | 3 | 4 | 5 | 6 | 7 | 8 | 9 | 10 | A |
| 5 | hit | hit | hit | hit | hit | hit | hit | hit | hit | hit |
| 6 | hit | hit | hit | hit | hit | hit | hit | hit | hit | hit |
| 7 | hit | hit | hit | hit | hit | hit | hit | hit | hit | hit |
| 8 | hit | hit | hit | hit | hit | hit | hit | hit | hit | hit |

| | 2 | 3 | 4 | 5 | 6 | 7 | 8 | 9 | 10 | A |
|---|---|---|---|---|---|---|---|---|---|---|
| 9 | hit | dd | dd | dd | dd | hit | hit | hit | hit | hit |
| 10 | dd | dd | dd | dd | dd | dd | dd | dd | hit | hit |
| 11 | dd | dd | dd | dd | dd | dd | dd | dd | dd | dd |
| 12 | hit | hit | st | st | st | hit | hit | hit | hit | hit |
| 13 | st | st | st | st | st | hit | hit | hit | hit | sur |
| 14 | st | st | st | st | st | hit | hit | hit | sur | sur |
| 15 | st | st | st | st | st | hit | hit | hit | sur | sur |
| 16 | st | st | st | st | st | hit | hit | sur | sur | sur |
| 17–21 | st | st | st | st | st | st | st | st | st | st |

## Soft Count — Dealer's Up Card

| Your Hand | 2 | 3 | 4 | 5 | 6 | 7 | 8 | 9 | 10 | A |
|---|---|---|---|---|---|---|---|---|---|---|
| soft 13 | hit | hit | hit | dd | dd | hit | hit | hit | hit | hit |
| soft 14 | hit | hit | hit | dd | dd | hit | hit | hit | hit | hit |
| soft 15 | hit | hit | dd | dd | dd | hit | hit | hit | hit | hit |
| soft 16 | hit | hit | dd | dd | dd | hit | hit | hit | hit | hit |
| soft 17 | hit | dd | dd | dd | dd | hit | hit | hit | hit | hit |
| soft 18 | dd | dd | dd | dd | dd | st | st | hit | hit | hit |
| soft 19,20 | st | st | st | st | st | st | st | st | st | st |

## Pairs — Dealer's Up Card

| Your Hand | 2 | 3 | 4 | 5 | 6 | 7 | 8 | 9 | 10 | A |
|---|---|---|---|---|---|---|---|---|---|---|
| 2,2 | hit | hit | sp | sp | sp | sp | hit | hit | hit | hit |
| 3,3 | hit | hit | sp | sp | sp | sp | hit | hit | hit | hit |
| 4,4 | hit | hit | hit | hit | hit | hit | hit | hit | hit | hit |
| 5,5 | dd | dd | dd | dd | dd | dd | dd | dd | hit | hit |
| 6,6 | hit | sp | sp | sp | sp | hit | hit | hit | hit | hit |
| 7,7 | sp | sp | sp | sp | sp | sp | hit | hit | sur | sur |
| 8,8 | sp | sp | sp | sp | sp | sp | sp | sp | sur& | sur& |
| 9,9 | sp | sp | sp | sp | sp | st | sp | sp | st | st |
| 10,10 | st | st | st | st | st | st | st | st | st | st |
| A,A | sp | sp | sp | sp | sp | sp | sp | sp | sp | sp |

# CHART 4

Eight decks

Dealer hits soft 17

Double down on 10 and 11 only

Doubling down after splitting is allowed

| **Hard count** | | | | **Dealer's Up Card** | | | | | | |
|---|---|---|---|---|---|---|---|---|---|---|
| Your Hand | 2 | 3 | 4 | 5 | 6 | 7 | 8 | 9 | 10 | A |
| 5 | hit | hit | hit | hit | hit | hit | hit | hit | hit | hit |
| 6 | hit | hit | hit | hit | hit | hit | hit | hit | hit | hit |
| 7 | hit | hit | hit | hit | hit | hit | hit | hit | hit | hit |
| 8 | hit | hit | hit | hit | hit | hit | hit | hit | hit | hit |
| 9 | hit | hit | hit | hit | hit | hit | hit | hit | hit | hit |
| 10 | dd | dd | dd | dd | dd | dd | dd | dd | hit | hit |
| 11 | dd | dd | dd | dd | dd | dd | dd | dd | dd | dd |
| 12 | hit | hit | st | st | st | hit | hit | hit | hit | hit |
| 13 | st | st | st | st | st | hit | hit | hit | hit | sur |
| 14 | st | st | st | st | st | hit | hit | hit | sur | sur |
| 15 | st | st | st | st | st | hit | hit | hit | sur | sur |
| 16 | st | st | st | st | st | hit | hit | sur | sur | sur |
| 17–21 | st | st | st | st | st | st | st | st | st | st |

| **Soft Count** | | | | **Dealer's Up Card** | | | | | | |
|---|---|---|---|---|---|---|---|---|---|---|
| Your Hand | 2 | 3 | 4 | 5 | 6 | 7 | 8 | 9 | 10 | A |
| soft 13 | hit | hit | hit | hit | hit | hit | hit | hit | hit | hit |
| soft 14 | hit | hit | hit | hit | hit | hit | hit | hit | hit | hit |
| soft 15 | hit | hit | hit | hit | hit | hit | hit | hit | hit | hit |
| soft 16 | hit | hit | hit | hit | hit | hit | hit | hit | hit | hit |
| soft 17 | hit | hit | hit | hit | hit | hit | hit | hit | hit | hit |
| soft 18 | st | st | st | st | st | st | st | hit | hit | hit |
| soft 19,20 | st | st | st | st | st | st | st | st | st | st |

**Pairs**            **Dealer's Up Card**

| Your Hand | 2 | 3 | 4 | 5 | 6 | 7 | 8 | 9 | 10 | A |
|---|---|---|---|---|---|---|---|---|---|---|
| 2,2 | sp | sp | sp | sp | sp | sp | hit | hit | hit | hit |
| 3,3 | sp | sp | sp | sp | sp | sp | hit | hit | hit | hit |
| 4,4 | hit | hit | hit | sp | sp | hit | hit | hit | hit | hit |
| 5,5 | dd | dd | dd | dd | dd | dd | dd | dd | hit | hit |
| 6,6 | sp | sp | sp | sp | sp | hit | hit | hit | hit | hit |
| 7,7 | sp | sp | sp | sp | sp | sp | hit | hit | sur | sur |
| 8,8 | sp | sp | sp | sp | sp | sp | sp | sp | sur& | sur& |
| 9,9 | sp | sp | sp | sp | sp | st | sp | sp | st | st |
| 10,10 | st | st | st | st | st | st | st | st | st | st |
| A,A | sp | sp | sp | sp | sp | sp | sp | sp | sp | sp |

# CHART 5

Eight decks

Dealer hits soft 17

Double down on 10 and 11 only

No doubling down after splitting

**Hard count**            **Dealer's Up Card**

| Your Hand | 2 | 3 | 4 | 5 | 6 | 7 | 8 | 9 | 10 | A |
|---|---|---|---|---|---|---|---|---|---|---|
| 5 | hit | hit | hit | hit | hit | hit | hit | hit | hit | hit |
| 6 | hit | hit | hit | hit | hit | hit | hit | hit | hit | hit |
| 7 | hit | hit | hit | hit | hit | hit | hit | hit | hit | hit |
| 8 | hit | hit | hit | hit | hit | hit | hit | hit | hit | hit |
| 9 | hit | hit | hit | hit | hit | hit | hit | hit | hit | hit |
| 10 | dd | dd | dd | dd | dd | dd | dd | dd | hit | hit |
| 11 | dd | dd | dd | dd | dd | dd | dd | dd | dd | dd |
| 12 | hit | hit | st | st | st | hit | hit | hit | hit | hit |
| 13 | st | st | st | st | st | hit | hit | hit | hit | sur |

| | | | | | | | | | | |
|---|---|---|---|---|---|---|---|---|---|---|
| 14 | st | st | st | st | st | hit | hit | hit | sur | sur |
| 15 | st | st | st | st | st | hit | hit | hit | sur | sur |
| 16 | st | st | st | st | st | hit | hit | sur | sur | sur |
| 17–21 | st | st | st | st | st | st | st | st | st | st |

## Soft Count — Dealer's Up Card

| Your Hand | 2 | 3 | 4 | 5 | 6 | 7 | 8 | 9 | 10 | A |
|---|---|---|---|---|---|---|---|---|---|---|
| soft 13 | hit | hit | hit | hit | hit | hit | hit | hit | hit | hit |
| soft 14 | hit | hit | hit | hit | hit | hit | hit | hit | hit | hit |
| soft 15 | hit | hit | hit | hit | hit | hit | hit | hit | hit | hit |
| soft 16 | hit | hit | hit | hit | hit | hit | hit | hit | hit | hit |
| soft 17 | hit | hit | hit | hit | hit | hit | hit | hit | hit | hit |
| soft 18 | st | st | st | st | st | st | st | hit | hit | hit |
| soft 19,20 | st | st | st | st | st | st | st | st | st | st |

## Pairs — Dealer's Up Card

| Your Hand | 2 | 3 | 4 | 5 | 6 | 7 | 8 | 9 | 10 | A |
|---|---|---|---|---|---|---|---|---|---|---|
| 2,2 | hit | hit | sp | sp | sp | sp | hit | hit | hit | hit |
| 3,3 | hit | hit | sp | sp | sp | sp | hit | hit | hit | hit |
| 4,4 | hit | hit | hit | hit | hit | hit | hit | hit | hit | hit |
| 5,5 | dd | dd | dd | dd | dd | dd | dd | dd | hit | hit |
| 6,6 | hit | sp | sp | sp | sp | hit | hit | hit | hit | hit |
| 7,7 | sp | sp | sp | sp | sp | sp | hit | hit | sur | sur |
| 8,8 | sp | sp | sp | sp | sp | sp | sp | sp | sur& | sur& |
| 9,9 | sp | sp | sp | sp | sp | st | sp | sp | st | st |
| 10,10 | st | st | st | st | st | st | st | st | st | st |
| A,A | sp | sp | sp | sp | sp | sp | sp | sp | sp | sp |

# CHART 6

Eight decks

Dealer stands on soft 17

Double down on any hand

Doubling down after splitting is allowed

## Hard count — Dealer's Up Card

| Your Hand | 2 | 3 | 4 | 5 | 6 | 7 | 8 | 9 | 10 | A |
|---|---|---|---|---|---|---|---|---|---|---|
| 5 | hit | hit | hit | hit | hit | hit | hit | hit | hit | hit |
| 6 | hit | hit | hit | hit | hit | hit | hit | hit | hit | hit |
| 7 | hit | hit | hit | hit | hit | hit | hit | hit | hit | hit |
| 8 | hit | hit | hit | hit | hit | hit | hit | hit | hit | hit |
| 9 | hit | dd | dd | dd | dd | hit | hit | hit | hit | hit |
| 10 | dd | dd | dd | dd | dd | dd | dd | dd | hit | hit |
| 11 | dd | dd | dd | dd | dd | dd | dd | dd | dd | hit |
| 12 | hit | hit | st | st | st | hit | hit | hit | hit | hit |
| 13 | st | st | st | st | st | hit | hit | hit | hit | sur |
| 14 | st | st | st | st | st | hit | hit | hit | sur | sur |
| 15 | st | st | st | st | st | hit | hit | hit | sur | sur |
| 16 | st | st | st | st | st | hit | hit | sur | sur | sur |
| 17–21 | st | st | st | st | st | st | st | st | st | st |

## Soft Count — Dealer's Up Card

| Your Hand | 2 | 3 | 4 | 5 | 6 | 7 | 8 | 9 | 10 | A |
|---|---|---|---|---|---|---|---|---|---|---|
| soft 13 | hit | hit | hit | dd | dd | hit | hit | hit | hit | hit |
| soft 14 | hit | hit | hit | dd | dd | hit | hit | hit | hit | hit |
| soft 15 | hit | hit | dd | dd | dd | hit | hit | hit | hit | hit |
| soft 16 | hit | hit | dd | dd | dd | hit | hit | hit | hit | hit |
| soft 17 | hit | dd | dd | dd | dd | hit | hit | hit | hit | hit |
| soft 18 | st | dd | dd | dd | dd | st | st | hit | hit | hit |
| soft 19,20 | st | st | st | st | st | st | st | st | st | st |

| Pairs | | | | Dealer's Up Card | | | | | | |
|---|---|---|---|---|---|---|---|---|---|---|
| Your Hand | 2 | 3 | 4 | 5 | 6 | 7 | 8 | 9 | 10 | A |
| 2,2 | sp | sp | sp | sp | sp | sp | hit | hit | hit | hit |
| 3,3 | sp | sp | sp | sp | sp | sp | hit | hit | hit | hit |
| 4,4 | hit | hit | hit | sp | sp | hit | hit | hit | hit | hit |
| 5,5 | dd | dd | dd | dd | dd | dd | dd | dd | hit | hit |
| 6,6 | sp | sp | sp | sp | sp | hit | hit | hit | hit | hit |
| 7,7 | sp | sp | sp | sp | sp | sp | hit | hit | sur | sur |
| 8,8 | sp | sp | sp | sp | sp | sp | sp | sp | sur& | sur |
| 9,9 | sp | sp | sp | sp | sp | st | sp | sp | st | st |
| 10,10 | st | st | st | st | st | st | st | st | st | st |
| A,A | sp | sp | sp | sp | sp | sp | sp | sp | sp | sp |

# CHART 7

Eight decks

Dealer stands on soft 17

Double down on 10 or 11 only

Doubling down after splitting is allowed

| Hard count | | | | Dealer's Up Card | | | | | | |
|---|---|---|---|---|---|---|---|---|---|---|
| Your Hand | 2 | 3 | 4 | 5 | 6 | 7 | 8 | 9 | 10 | A |
| 5 | hit | hit | hit | hit | hit | hit | hit | hit | hit | hit |
| 6 | hit | hit | hit | hit | hit | hit | hit | hit | hit | hit |
| 7 | hit | hit | hit | hit | hit | hit | hit | hit | hit | hit |
| 8 | hit | hit | hit | hit | hit | hit | hit | hit | hit | hit |
| 9 | hit | hit | hit | hit | hit | hit | hit | hit | hit | hit |
| 10 | dd | dd | dd | dd | dd | dd | dd | dd | hit | hit |
| 11 | dd | dd | dd | dd | dd | dd | dd | dd | dd | hit |
| 12 | hit | hit | st | st | st | hit | hit | hit | hit | hit |
| 13 | st | st | st | st | st | hit | hit | hit | hit | sur |
| 14 | st | st | st | st | st | hit | hit | hit | sur | sur |

| Your Hand | | | | | | | | | | |
|---|---|---|---|---|---|---|---|---|---|---|
| 15 | st | st | st | st | st | hit | hit | hit | sur | sur |
| 16 | st | st | st | st | st | hit | hit | sur | sur | sur |
| 17–21 | st | st | st | st | st | st | st | st | st | st |

## Soft Count — Dealer's Up Card

| Your Hand | 2 | 3 | 4 | 5 | 6 | 7 | 8 | 9 | 10 | A |
|---|---|---|---|---|---|---|---|---|---|---|
| soft 13 | hit | hit | hit | hit | hit | hit | hit | hit | hit | hit |
| soft 14 | hit | hit | hit | hit | hit | hit | hit | hit | hit | hit |
| soft 15 | hit | hit | hit | hit | hit | hit | hit | hit | hit | hit |
| soft 16 | hit | hit | hit | hit | hit | hit | hit | hit | hit | hit |
| soft 17 | hit | hit | hit | hit | hit | hit | hit | hit | hit | hit |
| soft 18 | st | st | st | st | st | st | st | hit | hit | hit |
| soft 19,20 | st | st | st | st | st | st | st | st | st | st |

## Pairs — Dealer's Up Card

| Your Hand | 2 | 3 | 4 | 5 | 6 | 7 | 8 | 9 | 10 | A |
|---|---|---|---|---|---|---|---|---|---|---|
| 2,2 | sp | sp | sp | sp | sp | sp | hit | hit | hit | hit |
| 3,3 | sp | sp | sp | sp | sp | sp | hit | hit | hit | hit |
| 4,4 | hit | hit | hit | sp | sp | hit | hit | hit | hit | hit |
| 5,5 | dd | dd | dd | dd | dd | dd | dd | dd | hit | hit |
| 6,6 | sp | sp | sp | sp | sp | hit | hit | hit | hit | hit |
| 7,7 | sp | sp | sp | sp | sp | sp | hit | hit | sur | sur |
| 8,8 | sp | sp | sp | sp | sp | sp | sp | sp | sur& | sur& |
| 9,9 | sp | sp | sp | sp | sp | st | sp | sp | st | st |
| 10,10 | st | st | st | st | st | st | st | st | st | st |
| A,A | sp | sp | sp | sp | sp | sp | sp | sp | sp | sp |

# CHART 8

Eight decks

Dealer stands on soft 17

Double down on 10 or 11 only

No doubling down after splitting

| Hard count | | | | Dealer's Up Card | | | | | | |
|---|---|---|---|---|---|---|---|---|---|---|
| Your Hand | 2 | 3 | 4 | 5 | 6 | 7 | 8 | 9 | 10 | A |
| 5 | hit | hit | hit | hit | hit | hit | hit | hit | hit | hit |
| 6 | hit | hit | hit | hit | hit | hit | hit | hit | hit | hit |
| 7 | hit | hit | hit | hit | hit | hit | hit | hit | hit | hit |
| 8 | hit | hit | hit | hit | hit | hit | hit | hit | hit | hit |
| 9 | hit | hit | hit | hit | hit | hit | hit | hit | hit | hit |
| 10 | dd | dd | dd | dd | dd | dd | dd | dd | hit | hit |
| 11 | dd | dd | dd | dd | dd | dd | dd | dd | dd | hit |
| 12 | hit | hit | st | st | st | hit | hit | hit | hit | hit |
| 13 | st | st | st | st | st | hit | hit | hit | hit | sur |
| 14 | st | st | st | st | st | hit | hit | hit | sur | sur |
| 15 | st | st | st | st | st | hit | hit | hit | sur | sur |
| 16 | st | st | st | st | st | hit | hit | sur | sur | sur |
| 17–21 | st | st | st | st | st | st | st | st | st | st |

| Soft Count | | | | Dealer's Up Card | | | | | | |
|---|---|---|---|---|---|---|---|---|---|---|
| Your Hand | 2 | 3 | 4 | 5 | 6 | 7 | 8 | 9 | 10 | A |
| soft 13 | hit | hit | hit | hit | hit | hit | hit | hit | hit | hit |
| soft 14 | hit | hit | hit | hit | hit | hit | hit | hit | hit | hit |
| soft 15 | hit | hit | hit | hit | hit | hit | hit | hit | hit | hit |
| soft 16 | hit | hit | hit | hit | hit | hit | hit | hit | hit | hit |
| soft 17 | hit | hit | hit | hit | hit | hit | hit | hit | hit | hit |
| soft 18 | st | st | st | st | st | st | st | hit | hit | hit |
| soft 19,20 | st | st | st | st | st | st | st | st | st | st |

| Pairs | | | | Dealer's Up Card | | | | | | |
|-------|---|---|---|---|---|---|---|---|---|---|
| Your Hand | 2 | 3 | 4 | 5 | 6 | 7 | 8 | 9 | 10 | A |
| 2,2 | hit | hit | sp | sp | sp | sp | hit | hit | hit | hit |
| 3,3 | hit | hit | sp | sp | sp | sp | hit | hit | hit | hit |
| 4,4 | hit | hit | hit | hit | hit | hit | hit | hit | hit | hit |
| 5,5 | dd | dd | dd | dd | dd | dd | dd | dd | hit | hit |
| 6,6 | hit | sp | sp | sp | sp | hit | hit | hit | hit | hit |
| 7,7 | sp | sp | sp | sp | sp | sp | hit | hit | sur | sur |
| 8,8 | sp | sp | sp | sp | sp | sp | sp | sp | sur& | sur& |
| 9,9 | sp | sp | sp | sp | sp | st | sp | sp | st | st |
| 10,10 | st | st | st | st | st | st | st | st | st | st |
| A,A | sp | sp | sp | sp | sp | sp | sp | sp | sp | sp |

# CHART 9

Six decks

Dealer hits soft 17

Double down on any hand

Doubling down after splitting is allowed

| Hard count | | | | Dealer's Up Card | | | | | | |
|-----------|---|---|---|---|---|---|---|---|---|---|
| Your Hand | 2 | 3 | 4 | 5 | 6 | 7 | 8 | 9 | 10 | A |
| 5 | hit | hit | hit | hit | hit | hit | hit | hit | hit | hit |
| 6 | hit | hit | hit | hit | hit | hit | hit | hit | hit | hit |
| 7 | hit | hit | hit | hit | hit | hit | hit | hit | hit | hit |
| 8 | hit | hit | hit | hit | hit | hit | hit | hit | hit | hit |
| 9 | hit | dd | dd | dd | dd | hit | hit | hit | hit | hit |
| 10 | dd | dd | dd | dd | dd | dd | dd | dd | hit | hit |
| 11 | dd | dd | dd | dd | dd | dd | dd | dd | dd | dd |
| 12 | hit | hit | st | st | st | hit | hit | hit | hit | hit |
| 13 | st | st | st | st | st | hit | hit | hit | hit | sur |

| 14 | st | st | st | st | st | hit | hit | hit | sur | sur |
| 15 | st | st | st | st | st | hit | hit | hit | sur | sur |
| 16 | st | st | st | st | st | hit | hit | sur | sur | sur |
| 17–21 | st | st | st | st | st | st | st | st | st | st |

## Soft Count · Dealer's Up Card

| Your Hand | 2 | 3 | 4 | 5 | 6 | 7 | 8 | 9 | 10 | A |
|---|---|---|---|---|---|---|---|---|---|---|
| soft 13 | hit | hit | hit | dd | dd | hit | hit | hit | hit | hit |
| soft 14 | hit | hit | hit | dd | dd | hit | hit | hit | hit | hit |
| soft 15 | hit | hit | dd | dd | dd | hit | hit | hit | hit | hit |
| soft 16 | hit | hit | dd | dd | dd | hit | hit | hit | hit | hit |
| soft 17 | hit | dd | dd | dd | dd | hit | hit | hit | hit | hit |
| soft 18 | dd | dd | dd | dd | dd | st | st | hit | hit | hit |
| soft 19,20 | st | st | st | st | st | st | st | st | st | st |

## Pairs · Dealer's Up Card

| Your Hand | 2 | 3 | 4 | 5 | 6 | 7 | 8 | 9 | 10 | A |
|---|---|---|---|---|---|---|---|---|---|---|
| 2,2 | sp | sp | sp | sp | sp | sp | hit | hit | hit | hit |
| 3,3 | sp | sp | sp | sp | sp | sp | hit | hit | hit | hit |
| 4,4 | hit | hit | hit | sp | sp | hit | hit | hit | hit | hit |
| 5,5 | dd | dd | dd | dd | dd | dd | dd | dd | hit | hit |
| 6,6 | sp | sp | sp | sp | sp | hit | hit | hit | hit | hit |
| 7,7 | sp | sp | sp | sp | sp | sp | hit | hit | sur | sur |
| 8,8 | sp | sp | sp | sp | sp | sp | sp | sp | sur& | sur& |
| 9,9 | sp | sp | sp | sp | sp | st | sp | sp | st | st |
| 10,10 | st | st | st | st | st | st | st | st | st | st |
| A,A | sp | sp | sp | sp | sp | sp | sp | sp | sp | sp |

# CHART 10

Six decks

Dealer hits soft 17

Double down on any hand

No doubling down after splitting

| Hard count | Dealer's Up Card | | | | | | | | | |
|---|---|---|---|---|---|---|---|---|---|---|
| Your Hand | 2 | 3 | 4 | 5 | 6 | 7 | 8 | 9 | 10 | A |
| 5 | hit | hit | hit | hit | hit | hit | hit | hit | hit | hit |
| 6 | hit | hit | hit | hit | hit | hit | hit | hit | hit | hit |
| 7 | hit | hit | hit | hit | hit | hit | hit | hit | hit | hit |
| 8 | hit | hit | hit | hit | hit | hit | hit | hit | hit | hit |
| 9 | hit | dd | dd | dd | dd | hit | hit | hit | hit | hit |
| 10 | dd | dd | dd | dd | dd | dd | dd | dd | hit | hit |
| 11 | dd | dd | dd | dd | dd | dd | dd | dd | dd | dd |
| 12 | hit | hit | st | st | st | hit | hit | hit | hit | hit |
| 13 | st | st | st | st | st | hit | hit | hit | hit | sur |
| 14 | st | st | st | st | st | hit | hit | hit | sur | sur |
| 15 | st | st | st | st | st | hit | hit | hit | sur | sur |
| 16 | st | st | st | st | st | hit | hit | sur | sur | sur |
| 17–21 | st | st | st | st | st | st | st | st | st | st |

| Soft Count | Dealer's Up Card | | | | | | | | | |
|---|---|---|---|---|---|---|---|---|---|---|
| Your Hand | 2 | 3 | 4 | 5 | 6 | 7 | 8 | 9 | 10 | A |
| soft 13 | hit | hit | hit | dd | dd | hit | hit | hit | hit | hit |
| soft 14 | hit | hit | hit | dd | dd | hit | hit | hit | hit | hit |
| soft 15 | hit | hit | dd | dd | dd | hit | hit | hit | hit | hit |
| soft 16 | hit | hit | dd | dd | dd | hit | hit | hit | hit | hit |
| soft 17 | hit | dd | dd | dd | dd | hit | hit | hit | hit | hit |
| soft 18 | dd | dd | dd | dd | dd | st | st | hit | hit | hit |
| soft 19,20 | st | st | st | st | st | st | st | st | st | st |

| Pairs | Dealer's Up Card | | | | | | | | | |
|---|---|---|---|---|---|---|---|---|---|---|
| Your Hand | 2 | 3 | 4 | 5 | 6 | 7 | 8 | 9 | 10 | A |
| 2,2 | hit | hit | sp | sp | sp | sp | hit | hit | hit | hit |
| 3,3 | hit | hit | sp | sp | sp | sp | hit | hit | hit | hit |
| 4,4 | hit | hit | hit | hit | hit | hit | hit | hit | hit | hit |
| 5,5 | dd | dd | dd | dd | dd | dd | dd | dd | hit | hit |
| 6,6 | hit | sp | sp | sp | sp | hit | hit | hit | hit | hit |
| 7,7 | sp | sp | sp | sp | sp | sp | hit | hit | sur | sur |
| 8,8 | sp | sp | sp | sp | sp | sp | sp | sp | sur& | sur& |
| 9,9 | sp | sp | sp | sp | sp | st | sp | sp | st | st |
| 10,10 | st | st | st | st | st | st | st | st | st | st |
| A,A | sp | sp | sp | sp | sp | sp | sp | sp | sp | sp |

# CHART 11

Six decks

Dealer hits soft 17

Double down on 10 or 11 only

Doubling down after splitting is allowed

| Hard count | Dealer's Up Card | | | | | | | | | |
|---|---|---|---|---|---|---|---|---|---|---|
| Your Hand | 2 | 3 | 4 | 5 | 6 | 7 | 8 | 9 | 10 | A |
| 5 | hit | hit | hit | hit | hit | hit | hit | hit | hit | hit |
| 6 | hit | hit | hit | hit | hit | hit | hit | hit | hit | hit |
| 7 | hit | hit | hit | hit | hit | hit | hit | hit | hit | hit |
| 8 | hit | hit | hit | hit | hit | hit | hit | hit | hit | hit |
| 9 | hit | hit | hit | hit | hit | hit | hit | hit | hit | hit |
| 10 | dd | dd | dd | dd | dd | dd | dd | dd | hit | hit |
| 11 | dd | dd | dd | dd | dd | dd | dd | dd | dd | dd |
| 12 | hit | hit | st | st | st | hit | hit | hit | hit | hit |
| 13 | st | st | st | st | st | hit | hit | hit | hit | sur |
| 14 | st | st | st | st | st | hit | hit | hit | sur | sur |

| | | | | | | | | | | |
|---|---|---|---|---|---|---|---|---|---|---|
| 15 | st | st | st | st | st | hit | hit | hit | sur | sur |
| 16 | st | st | st | st | st | hit | hit | sur | sur | sur |
| 17–21 | st | st | st | st | st | st | st | st | st | st |

## Soft Count                    Dealer's Up Card

| Your Hand | 2 | 3 | 4 | 5 | 6 | 7 | 8 | 9 | 10 | A |
|---|---|---|---|---|---|---|---|---|---|---|
| soft 13 | hit | hit | hit | hit | hit | hit | hit | hit | hit | hit |
| soft 14 | hit | hit | hit | hit | hit | hit | hit | hit | hit | hit |
| soft 15 | hit | hit | hit | hit | hit | hit | hit | hit | hit | hit |
| soft 16 | hit | hit | hit | hit | hit | hit | hit | hit | hit | hit |
| soft 17 | hit | hit | hit | hit | hit | hit | hit | hit | hit | hit |
| soft 18 | st | st | st | st | st | st | st | hit | hit | hit |
| soft 19,20 | st | st | st | st | st | st | st | st | st | st |

## Pairs                    Dealer's Up Card

| Your Hand | 2 | 3 | 4 | 5 | 6 | 7 | 8 | 9 | 10 | A |
|---|---|---|---|---|---|---|---|---|---|---|
| 2,2 | sp | sp | sp | sp | sp | sp | hit | hit | hit | hit |
| 3,3 | sp | sp | sp | sp | sp | sp | hit | hit | hit | hit |
| 4,4 | hit | hit | hit | sp | sp | hit | hit | hit | hit | hit |
| 5,5 | dd | dd | dd | dd | dd | dd | dd | dd | hit | hit |
| 6,6 | sp | sp | sp | sp | sp | hit | hit | hit | hit | hit |
| 7,7 | sp | sp | sp | sp | sp | sp | hit | hit | sur | sur |
| 8,8 | sp | sp | sp | sp | sp | sp | sp | sp | sur& | sur& |
| 9,9 | sp | sp | sp | sp | sp | st | sp | sp | st | st |
| 10,10 | st | st | st | st | st | st | st | st | st | st |
| A,A | sp | sp | sp | sp | sp | sp | sp | sp | sp | sp |

# CHART 12

Six decks

Dealer hits soft 17

Double down on 10 or 11 only

No doubling down after splitting

**Hard count**                                     **Dealer's Up Card**

| Your Hand | 2 | 3 | 4 | 5 | 6 | 7 | 8 | 9 | 10 | A |
|---|---|---|---|---|---|---|---|---|---|---|
| 5 | hit | hit | hit | hit | hit | hit | hit | hit | hit | hit |
| 6 | hit | hit | hit | hit | hit | hit | hit | hit | hit | hit |
| 7 | hit | hit | hit | hit | hit | hit | hit | hit | hit | hit |
| 8 | hit | hit | hit | hit | hit | hit | hit | hit | hit | hit |
| 9 | hit | hit | hit | hit | hit | hit | hit | hit | hit | hit |
| 10 | dd | dd | dd | dd | dd | dd | dd | dd | hit | hit |
| 11 | dd | dd | dd | dd | dd | dd | dd | dd | dd | dd |
| 12 | hit | hit | st | st | st | hit | hit | hit | hit | hit |
| 13 | st | st | st | st | st | hit | hit | hit | hit | sur |
| 14 | st | st | st | st | st | hit | hit | hit | sur | sur |
| 15 | st | st | st | st | st | hit | hit | hit | sur | sur |
| 16 | st | st | st | st | st | hit | hit | sur | sur | sur |
| 17–21 | st | st | st | st | st | st | st | st | st | st |

**Soft Count**                                      **Dealer's Up Card**

| Your Hand | 2 | 3 | 4 | 5 | 6 | 7 | 8 | 9 | 10 | A |
|---|---|---|---|---|---|---|---|---|---|---|
| soft 13 | hit | hit | hit | hit | hit | hit | hit | hit | hit | hit |
| soft 14 | hit | hit | hit | hit | hit | hit | hit | hit | hit | hit |
| soft 15 | hit | hit | hit | hit | hit | hit | hit | hit | hit | hit |
| soft 16 | hit | hit | hit | hit | hit | hit | hit | hit | hit | hit |
| soft 17 | hit | hit | hit | hit | hit | hit | hit | hit | hit | hit |
| soft 18 | st | st | st | st | st | st | st | hit | hit | hit |
| soft 19,20 | st | st | st | st | st | st | st | st | st | st |

**Pairs** — **Dealer's Up Card**

| Your Hand | 2 | 3 | 4 | 5 | 6 | 7 | 8 | 9 | 10 | A |
|---|---|---|---|---|---|---|---|---|---|---|
| 2,2 | hit | hit | sp | sp | sp | sp | hit | hit | hit | hit |
| 3,3 | hit | hit | sp | sp | sp | sp | hit | hit | hit | hit |
| 4,4 | hit | hit | hit | hit | hit | hit | hit | hit | hit | hit |
| 5,5 | dd | dd | dd | dd | dd | dd | dd | dd | hit | hit |
| 6,6 | hit | sp | sp | sp | sp | hit | hit | hit | hit | hit |
| 7,7 | sp | sp | sp | sp | sp | sp | hit | hit | sur | sur |
| 8,8 | sp | sp | sp | sp | sp | sp | sp | sp | sur& | sur& |
| 9,9 | sp | sp | sp | sp | sp | st | sp | sp | st | st |
| 10,10 | st | st | st | st | st | st | st | st | st | st |
| A,A | sp | sp | sp | sp | sp | sp | sp | sp | sp | sp |

# CHART 13

Six decks

Dealer stands on soft 17

Double down on any hand

Doubling down after splitting is allowed

**Hard count** — **Dealer's Up Card**

| Your Hand | 2 | 3 | 4 | 5 | 6 | 7 | 8 | 9 | 10 | A |
|---|---|---|---|---|---|---|---|---|---|---|
| 5 | hit | hit | hit | hit | hit | hit | hit | hit | hit | hit |
| 6 | hit | hit | hit | hit | hit | hit | hit | hit | hit | hit |
| 7 | hit | hit | hit | hit | hit | hit | hit | hit | hit | hit |
| 8 | hit | hit | hit | hit | hit | hit | hit | hit | hit | hit |
| 9 | hit | dd | dd | dd | dd | hit | hit | hit | hit | hit |
| 10 | dd | dd | dd | dd | dd | dd | dd | dd | hit | hit |
| 11 | dd | dd | dd | dd | dd | dd | dd | dd | dd | hit |
| 12 | hit | hit | st | st | st | hit | hit | hit | hit | hit |
| 13 | st | st | st | st | st | hit | hit | hit | hit | sur |

| | | | | | | | | | | |
|---|---|---|---|---|---|---|---|---|---|---|
| 14 | st | st | st | st | st | hit | hit | hit | sur | sur |
| 15 | st | st | st | st | st | hit | hit | hit | sur | sur |
| 16 | st | st | st | st | st | hit | hit | sur | sur | sur |
| 17–21 | st | st | st | st | st | st | st | st | st | st |

## Soft Count

| Your Hand | 2 | 3 | 4 | 5 | 6 | 7 | 8 | 9 | 10 | A |
|---|---|---|---|---|---|---|---|---|---|---|
| | | | | Dealer's Up Card | | | | | | |
| soft 13 | hit | hit | hit | dd | dd | hit | hit | hit | hit | hit |
| soft 14 | hit | hit | hit | dd | dd | hit | hit | hit | hit | hit |
| soft 15 | hit | hit | dd | dd | dd | hit | hit | hit | hit | hit |
| soft 16 | hit | hit | dd | dd | dd | hit | hit | hit | hit | hit |
| soft 17 | hit | dd | dd | dd | dd | hit | hit | hit | hit | hit |
| soft 18 | st | dd | dd | dd | dd | st | st | hit | hit | hit |
| soft 19,20 | st | st | st | st | st | st | st | st | st | st |

## Pairs

| Your Hand | 2 | 3 | 4 | 5 | 6 | 7 | 8 | 9 | 10 | A |
|---|---|---|---|---|---|---|---|---|---|---|
| | | | | Dealer's Up Card | | | | | | |
| 2,2 | sp | sp | sp | sp | sp | sp | hit | hit | hit | hit |
| 3,3 | sp | sp | sp | sp | sp | sp | hit | hit | hit | hit |
| 4,4 | hit | hit | hit | sp | sp | hit | hit | hit | hit | hit |
| 5,5 | dd | dd | dd | dd | dd | dd | dd | dd | hit | hit |
| 6,6 | sp | sp | sp | sp | sp | hit | hit | hit | hit | hit |
| 7,7 | sp | sp | sp | sp | sp | sp | hit | hit | sur | sur |
| 8,8 | sp | sp | sp | sp | sp | sp | sp | sp | sur& | sur& |
| 9,9 | sp | sp | sp | sp | sp | st | sp | sp | st | st |
| 10,10 | st | st | st | st | st | st | st | st | st | st |
| A,A | sp | sp | sp | sp | sp | sp | sp | sp | sp | sp |

# CHART 14

Six decks

Dealer stands on soft 17

Double down on any hand

No doubling down after splitting

**Hard count**                   **Dealer's Up Card**

| Your Hand | 2 | 3 | 4 | 5 | 6 | 7 | 8 | 9 | 10 | A |
|---|---|---|---|---|---|---|---|---|---|---|
| 5 | hit | hit | hit | hit | hit | hit | hit | hit | hit | hit |
| 6 | hit | hit | hit | hit | hit | hit | hit | hit | hit | hit |
| 7 | hit | hit | hit | hit | hit | hit | hit | hit | hit | hit |
| 8 | hit | hit | hit | hit | hit | hit | hit | hit | hit | hit |
| 9 | hit | dd | dd | dd | dd | hit | hit | hit | hit | hit |
| 10 | dd | dd | dd | dd | dd | dd | dd | dd | hit | hit |
| 11 | dd | dd | dd | dd | dd | dd | dd | dd | dd | hit |
| 12 | hit | hit | st | st | st | hit | hit | hit | hit | hit |
| 13 | st | st | st | st | st | hit | hit | hit | hit | sur |
| 14 | st | st | st | st | st | hit | hit | hit | sur | sur |
| 15 | st | st | st | st | st | hit | hit | hit | sur | sur |
| 16 | st | st | st | st | st | hit | hit | sur | sur | sur |
| 17–21 | st | st | st | st | st | st | st | st | st | st |

**Soft Count**                   **Dealer's Up Card**

| Your Hand | 2 | 3 | 4 | 5 | 6 | 7 | 8 | 9 | 10 | A |
|---|---|---|---|---|---|---|---|---|---|---|
| soft 13 | hit | hit | hit | dd | dd | hit | hit | hit | hit | hit |
| soft 14 | hit | hit | hit | dd | dd | hit | hit | hit | hit | hit |
| soft 15 | hit | hit | dd | dd | dd | hit | hit | hit | hit | hit |
| soft 16 | hit | hit | dd | dd | dd | hit | hit | hit | hit | hit |
| soft 17 | hit | dd | dd | dd | dd | hit | hit | hit | hit | hit |
| soft 18 | st | dd | dd | dd | dd | st | st | hit | hit | hit |
| soft 19,20 | st | st | st | st | st | st | st | st | st | st |

| Pairs | Dealer's Up Card | | | | | | | | | |
|---|---|---|---|---|---|---|---|---|---|---|
| Your Hand | 2 | 3 | 4 | 5 | 6 | 7 | 8 | 9 | 10 | A |
| 2,2 | hit | hit | sp | sp | sp | sp | hit | hit | hit | hit |
| 3,3 | hit | hit | sp | sp | sp | sp | hit | hit | hit | hit |
| 4,4 | hit | hit | hit | hit | hit | hit | hit | hit | hit | hit |
| 5,5 | dd | dd | dd | dd | dd | dd | dd | dd | hit | hit |
| 6,6 | hit | sp | sp | sp | sp | hit | hit | hit | hit | hit |
| 7,7 | sp | sp | sp | sp | sp | sp | hit | hit | sur | sur |
| 8,8 | sp | sp | sp | sp | sp | sp | sp | sp | sur& | sur& |
| 9,9 | sp | sp | sp | sp | sp | st | sp | sp | st | st |
| 10,10 | st | st | st | st | st | st | st | st | st | st |
| A,A | sp | sp | sp | sp | sp | sp | sp | sp | sp | sp |

## CHART 15

Six decks

Dealer stands on soft 17

Double down on 10 and 11 only

Doubling down after splitting is allowed

| Hard count | Dealer's Up Card | | | | | | | | | |
|---|---|---|---|---|---|---|---|---|---|---|
| Your Hand | 2 | 3 | 4 | 5 | 6 | 7 | 8 | 9 | 10 | A |
| 5 | hit | hit | hit | hit | hit | hit | hit | hit | hit | hit |
| 6 | hit | hit | hit | hit | hit | hit | hit | hit | hit | hit |
| 7 | hit | hit | hit | hit | hit | hit | hit | hit | hit | hit |
| 8 | hit | hit | hit | hit | hit | hit | hit | hit | hit | hit |
| 9 | hit | hit | hit | hit | hit | hit | hit | hit | hit | hit |
| 10 | dd | dd | dd | dd | dd | dd | dd | dd | hit | hit |
| 11 | dd | dd | dd | dd | dd | dd | dd | dd | dd | hit |
| 12 | hit | hit | st | st | st | hit | hit | hit | hit | hit |
| 13 | st | st | st | st | st | hit | hit | hit | hit | sur |
| 14 | st | st | st | st | st | hit | hit | hit | sur | sur |

| 15 | st | st | st | st | st | hit | hit | hit | sur | sur |
|----|----|----|----|----|----|-----|-----|-----|-----|-----|
| 16 | st | st | st | st | st | hit | hit | sur | sur | sur |
| 17–21 | st | st | st | st | st | st | st | st | st | st |

**Soft Count** — **Dealer's Up Card**

| Your Hand | 2 | 3 | 4 | 5 | 6 | 7 | 8 | 9 | 10 | A |
|-----------|---|---|---|---|---|---|---|---|----|---|
| soft 13 | hit | hit | hit | hit | hit | hit | hit | hit | hit | hit |
| soft 14 | hit | hit | hit | hit | hit | hit | hit | hit | hit | hit |
| soft 15 | hit | hit | hit | hit | hit | hit | hit | hit | hit | hit |
| soft 16 | hit | hit | hit | hit | hit | hit | hit | hit | hit | hit |
| soft 17 | hit | hit | hit | hit | hit | hit | hit | hit | hit | hit |
| soft 18 | st | st | st | st | st | st | st | hit | hit | hit |
| soft 19,20 | st | st | st | st | st | st | st | st | st | st |

**Pairs** — **Dealer's Up Card**

| Your Hand | 2 | 3 | 4 | 5 | 6 | 7 | 8 | 9 | 10 | A |
|-----------|---|---|---|---|---|---|---|---|----|---|
| 2,2 | sp | sp | sp | sp | sp | sp | hit | hit | hit | hit |
| 3,3 | sp | sp | sp | sp | sp | sp | hit | hit | hit | hit |
| 4,4 | hit | hit | hit | sp | sp | hit | hit | hit | hit | hit |
| 5,5 | dd | dd | dd | dd | dd | dd | dd | dd | hit | hit |
| 6,6 | sp | sp | sp | sp | sp | hit | hit | hit | hit | hit |
| 7,7 | sp | sp | sp | sp | sp | sp | hit | hit | sur | sur |
| 8,8 | sp | sp | sp | sp | sp | sp | sp | sp | sur& | sur& |
| 9,9 | sp | sp | sp | sp | sp | st | sp | sp | st | st |
| 10,10 | st | st | st | st | st | st | st | st | st | st |
| A,A | sp | sp | sp | sp | sp | sp | sp | sp | sp | sp |

# CHART 16

Six decks

Dealer stands on soft 17

Double down on 10 and 11 only

No doubling down after splitting

| Hard count | | | | Dealer's Up Card | | | | | | |
|---|---|---|---|---|---|---|---|---|---|---|
| Your Hand | 2 | 3 | 4 | 5 | 6 | 7 | 8 | 9 | 10 | A |
| 5 | hit | hit | hit | hit | hit | hit | hit | hit | hit | hit |
| 6 | hit | hit | hit | hit | hit | hit | hit | hit | hit | hit |
| 7 | hit | hit | hit | hit | hit | hit | hit | hit | hit | hit |
| 8 | hit | hit | hit | hit | hit | hit | hit | hit | hit | hit |
| 9 | hit | hit | hit | hit | hit | hit | hit | hit | hit | hit |
| 10 | dd | dd | dd | dd | dd | dd | dd | dd | hit | hit |
| 11 | dd | dd | dd | dd | dd | dd | dd | dd | dd | hit |
| 12 | hit | hit | st | st | st | hit | hit | hit | hit | hit |
| 13 | st | st | st | st | st | hit | hit | hit | hit | sur |
| 14 | st | st | st | st | st | hit | hit | hit | sur | sur |
| 15 | st | st | st | st | st | hit | hit | hit | sur | sur |
| 16 | st | st | st | st | st | hit | hit | sur | sur | sur |
| 17–21 | st | st | st | st | st | st | st | st | st | st |

| Soft Count | | | | Dealer's Up Card | | | | | | |
|---|---|---|---|---|---|---|---|---|---|---|
| Your Hand | 2 | 3 | 4 | 5 | 6 | 7 | 8 | 9 | 10 | A |
| soft 13 | hit | hit | hit | hit | hit | hit | hit | hit | hit | hit |
| soft 14 | hit | hit | hit | hit | hit | hit | hit | hit | hit | hit |
| soft 15 | hit | hit | hit | hit | hit | hit | hit | hit | hit | hit |
| soft 16 | hit | hit | hit | hit | hit | hit | hit | hit | hit | hit |
| soft 17 | hit | hit | hit | hit | hit | hit | hit | hit | hit | hit |
| soft 18 | st | st | st | st | st | st | st | hit | hit | hit |
| soft 19,20 | st | st | st | st | st | st | st | st | st | st |

**Pairs** **Dealer's Up Card**

| Your Hand | 2 | 3 | 4 | 5 | 6 | 7 | 8 | 9 | 10 | A |
|-----------|------|------|------|------|------|------|------|------|------|------|
| 2,2 | hit | hit | sp | sp | sp | sp | hit | hit | hit | hit |
| 3,3 | hit | hit | sp | sp | sp | sp | hit | hit | hit | hit |
| 4,4 | hit | hit | hit | hit | hit | hit | hit | hit | hit | hit |
| 5,5 | dd | dd | dd | dd | dd | dd | dd | dd | hit | hit |
| 6,6 | hit | sp | sp | sp | sp | hit | hit | hit | hit | hit |
| 7,7 | sp | sp | sp | sp | sp | sp | hit | hit | sur | sur |
| 8,8 | sp | sp | sp | sp | sp | sp | sp | sp | sur& | sur& |
| 9,9 | sp | sp | sp | sp | sp | st | sp | sp | st | st |
| 10,10 | st | st | st | st | st | st | st | st | st | st |
| A,A | sp | sp | sp | sp | sp | sp | sp | sp | sp | sp |

## CHART 17

Four decks

Dealer hits soft 17

Double down on any hand

Doubling down after splitting is allowed

**Hard count** **Dealer's Up Card**

| Your Hand | 2 | 3 | 4 | 5 | 6 | 7 | 8 | 9 | 10 | A |
|-----------|------|------|------|------|------|------|------|------|------|------|
| 5 | hit | hit | hit | hit | hit | hit | hit | hit | hit | hit |
| 6 | hit | hit | hit | hit | hit | hit | hit | hit | hit | hit |
| 7 | hit | hit | hit | hit | hit | hit | hit | hit | hit | hit |
| 8 | hit | hit | hit | hit | hit | hit | hit | hit | hit | hit |
| 9 | hit | dd | dd | dd | dd | hit | hit | hit | hit | hit |
| 10 | dd | dd | dd | dd | dd | dd | dd | dd | hit | hit |
| 11 | dd | dd | dd | dd | dd | dd | dd | dd | dd | dd |
| 12 | hit | hit | st | st | st | hit | hit | hit | hit | hit |
| 13 | st | st | st | st | st | hit | hit | hit | hit | sur |

| | | | | | | | | | | |
|---|---|---|---|---|---|---|---|---|---|---|
| 14 | st | st | st | st | st | hit | hit | hit | sur | sur |
| 15 | st | st | st | st | st | hit | hit | hit | sur | sur |
| 16 | st | st | st | st | st | hit | hit | sur | sur | sur |
| 17–21 | st | st | st | st | st | st | st | st | st | st |

| **Soft Count** | | | | | **Dealer's Up Card** | | | | | |
|---|---|---|---|---|---|---|---|---|---|---|
| Your Hand | 2 | 3 | 4 | 5 | 6 | 7 | 8 | 9 | 10 | A |
| soft 13 | hit | hit | hit | dd | dd | hit | hit | hit | hit | hit |
| soft 14 | hit | hit | hit | dd | dd | hit | hit | hit | hit | hit |
| soft 15 | hit | hit | dd | dd | dd | hit | hit | hit | hit | hit |
| soft 16 | hit | hit | dd | dd | dd | hit | hit | hit | hit | hit |
| soft 17 | hit | dd | dd | dd | dd | hit | hit | hit | hit | hit |
| soft 18 | dd | dd | dd | dd | dd | st | st | hit | hit | hit |
| soft 19,20 | st | st | st | st | st | st | st | st | st | st |

| **Pairs** | | | | | **Dealer's Up Card** | | | | | |
|---|---|---|---|---|---|---|---|---|---|---|
| Your Hand | 2 | 3 | 4 | 5 | 6 | 7 | 8 | 9 | 10 | A |
| 2,2 | sp | sp | sp | sp | sp | sp | hit | hit | hit | hit |
| 3,3 | sp | sp | sp | sp | sp | sp | hit | hit | hit | hit |
| 4,4 | hit | hit | hit | sp | sp | hit | hit | hit | hit | hit |
| 5,5 | dd | dd | dd | dd | dd | dd | dd | dd | hit | hit |
| 6,6 | sp | sp | sp | sp | sp | hit | hit | hit | hit | hit |
| 7,7 | sp | sp | sp | sp | sp | sp | hit | hit | sur | sur |
| 8,8 | sp | sp | sp | sp | sp | sp | sp | sp | sur& | sur& |
| 9,9 | sp | sp | sp | sp | sp | st | sp | sp | st | st |
| 10,10 | st | st | st | st | st | st | st | st | st | st |
| A,A | sp | sp | sp | sp | sp | sp | sp | sp | sp | sp |

# CHART 18

Four decks

Dealer hits soft 17

Double down on any hand

No doubling down after splitting

| Hard count | Dealer's Up Card | | | | | | | | | |
|---|---|---|---|---|---|---|---|---|---|---|
| Your Hand | 2 | 3 | 4 | 5 | 6 | 7 | 8 | 9 | 10 | A |
| 5 | hit | hit | hit | hit | hit | hit | hit | hit | hit | hit |
| 6 | hit | hit | hit | hit | hit | hit | hit | hit | hit | hit |
| 7 | hit | hit | hit | hit | hit | hit | hit | hit | hit | hit |
| 8 | hit | hit | hit | hit | hit | hit | hit | hit | hit | hit |
| 9 | hit | dd | dd | dd | dd | hit | hit | hit | hit | hit |
| 10 | dd | dd | dd | dd | dd | dd | dd | dd | hit | hit |
| 11 | dd | dd | dd | dd | dd | dd | dd | dd | dd | dd |
| 12 | hit | hit | st | st | st | hit | hit | hit | hit | hit |
| 13 | st | st | st | st | st | hit | hit | hit | hit | sur |
| 14 | st | st | st | st | st | hit | hit | hit | sur | sur |
| 15 | st | st | st | st | st | hit | hit | hit | sur | sur |
| 16 | st | st | st | st | st | hit | hit | sur | sur | sur |
| 17–21 | st | st | st | st | st | st | st | st | st | st |

| Soft Count | Dealer's Up Card | | | | | | | | | |
|---|---|---|---|---|---|---|---|---|---|---|
| Your Hand | 2 | 3 | 4 | 5 | 6 | 7 | 8 | 9 | 10 | A |
| soft 13 | hit | hit | hit | dd | dd | hit | hit | hit | hit | hit |
| soft 14 | hit | hit | hit | dd | dd | hit | hit | hit | hit | hit |
| soft 15 | hit | hit | dd | dd | dd | hit | hit | hit | hit | hit |
| soft 16 | hit | hit | dd | dd | dd | hit | hit | hit | hit | hit |
| soft 17 | hit | dd | dd | dd | dd | hit | hit | hit | hit | hit |
| soft 18 | dd | dd | dd | dd | dd | st | st | hit | hit | hit |
| soft 19,20 | st | st | st | st | st | st | st | st | st | st |

| Pairs | | | | Dealer's Up Card | | | | | | |
|---|---|---|---|---|---|---|---|---|---|---|
| Your Hand | 2 | 3 | 4 | 5 | 6 | 7 | 8 | 9 | 10 | A |
| 2,2 | hit | hit | sp | sp | sp | sp | hit | hit | hit | hit |
| 3,3 | hit | hit | sp | sp | sp | sp | hit | hit | hit | hit |
| 4,4 | hit | hit | hit | hit | hit | hit | hit | hit | hit | hit |
| 5,5 | dd | dd | dd | dd | dd | dd | dd | dd | hit | hit |
| 6,6 | hit | sp | sp | sp | sp | hit | hit | hit | hit | hit |
| 7,7 | sp | sp | sp | sp | sp | sp | hit | hit | sur | sur |
| 8,8 | sp | sp | sp | sp | sp | sp | sp | sp | sur& | sur& |
| 9,9 | sp | sp | sp | sp | sp | st | sp | sp | st | st |
| 10,10 | st | st | st | st | st | st | st | st | st | st |
| A,A | sp | sp | sp | sp | sp | sp | sp | sp | sp | sp |

## CHART 19

Four decks

Dealer hits soft 17

Double down on 10 or 11 only

Doubling down after splitting is allowed

| Hard count | | | | Dealer's Up Card | | | | | | |
|---|---|---|---|---|---|---|---|---|---|---|
| Your Hand | 2 | 3 | 4 | 5 | 6 | 7 | 8 | 9 | 10 | A |
| 5 | hit | hit | hit | hit | hit | hit | hit | hit | hit | hit |
| 6 | hit | hit | hit | hit | hit | hit | hit | hit | hit | hit |
| 7 | hit | hit | hit | hit | hit | hit | hit | hit | hit | hit |
| 8 | hit | hit | hit | hit | hit | hit | hit | hit | hit | hit |
| 9 | hit | hit | hit | hit | hit | hit | hit | hit | hit | hit |
| 10 | dd | dd | dd | dd | dd | dd | dd | dd | hit | hit |
| 11 | dd | dd | dd | dd | dd | dd | dd | dd | dd | dd |
| 12 | hit | hit | st | st | st | hit | hit | hit | hit | hit |
| 13 | st | st | st | st | st | hit | hit | hit | hit | sur |
| 14 | st | st | st | st | st | hit | hit | hit | sur | sur |

| | 2 | 3 | 4 | 5 | 6 | 7 | 8 | 9 | 10 | A |
|---|---|---|---|---|---|---|---|---|---|---|
| 15 | st | st | st | st | st | hit | hit | hit | sur | sur |
| 16 | st | st | st | st | st | hit | hit | sur | sur | sur |
| 17–21 | st | st | st | st | st | st | st | st | st | st |

**Soft Count**

| Your Hand | | | | | Dealer's Up Card | | | | | |
|---|---|---|---|---|---|---|---|---|---|---|
| | 2 | 3 | 4 | 5 | 6 | 7 | 8 | 9 | 10 | A |
| soft 13 | hit | hit | hit | hit | hit | hit | hit | hit | hit | hit |
| soft 14 | hit | hit | hit | hit | hit | hit | hit | hit | hit | hit |
| soft 15 | hit | hit | hit | hit | hit | hit | hit | hit | hit | hit |
| soft 16 | hit | hit | hit | hit | hit | hit | hit | hit | hit | hit |
| soft 17 | hit | hit | hit | hit | hit | hit | hit | hit | hit | hit |
| soft 18 | st | st | st | st | st | st | st | hit | hit | hit |
| soft 19,20 | st | st | st | st | st | st | st | st | st | st |

**Pairs**

| Your Hand | | | | | Dealer's Up Card | | | | | |
|---|---|---|---|---|---|---|---|---|---|---|
| | 2 | 3 | 4 | 5 | 6 | 7 | 8 | 9 | 10 | A |
| 2,2 | sp | sp | sp | sp | sp | sp | hit | hit | hit | hit |
| 3,3 | sp | sp | sp | sp | sp | sp | hit | hit | hit | hit |
| 4,4 | hit | hit | hit | sp | sp | hit | hit | hit | hit | hit |
| 5,5 | dd | dd | dd | dd | dd | dd | dd | dd | hit | hit |
| 6,6 | sp | sp | sp | sp | sp | hit | hit | hit | hit | hit |
| 7,7 | sp | sp | sp | sp | sp | sp | hit | hit | sur | sur |
| 8,8 | sp | sp | sp | sp | sp | sp | sp | sp | sur& | sur& |
| 9,9 | sp | sp | sp | sp | sp | st | sp | sp | st | st |
| 10,10 | st | st | st | st | st | st | st | st | st | st |
| A,A | sp | sp | sp | sp | sp | sp | sp | sp | sp | sp |

# CHART 20

Four decks

Dealer hits soft 17

Double down on 10 or 11 only

No doubling down after splitting

| Hard count | | | | Dealer's Up Card | | | | | | |
|---|---|---|---|---|---|---|---|---|---|---|
| Your Hand | 2 | 3 | 4 | 5 | 6 | 7 | 8 | 9 | 10 | A |
| 5 | hit | hit | hit | hit | hit | hit | hit | hit | hit | hit |
| 6 | hit | hit | hit | hit | hit | hit | hit | hit | hit | hit |
| 7 | hit | hit | hit | hit | hit | hit | hit | hit | hit | hit |
| 8 | hit | hit | hit | hit | hit | hit | hit | hit | hit | hit |
| 9 | hit | hit | hit | hit | hit | hit | hit | hit | hit | hit |
| 10 | dd | dd | dd | dd | dd | dd | dd | dd | hit | hit |
| 11 | dd | dd | dd | dd | dd | dd | dd | dd | dd | dd |
| 12 | hit | hit | st | st | st | hit | hit | hit | hit | hit |
| 13 | st | st | st | st | st | hit | hit | hit | hit | sur |
| 14 | st | st | st | st | st | hit | hit | hit | sur | sur |
| 15 | st | st | st | st | st | hit | hit | hit | sur | sur |
| 16 | st | st | st | st | st | hit | hit | sur | sur | sur |
| 17–21 | st | st | st | st | st | st | st | st | st | st |

| Soft Count | | | | Dealer's Up Card | | | | | | |
|---|---|---|---|---|---|---|---|---|---|---|
| Your Hand | 2 | 3 | 4 | 5 | 6 | 7 | 8 | 9 | 10 | A |
| soft 13 | hit | hit | hit | hit | hit | hit | hit | hit | hit | hit |
| soft 14 | hit | hit | hit | hit | hit | hit | hit | hit | hit | hit |
| soft 15 | hit | hit | hit | hit | hit | hit | hit | hit | hit | hit |
| soft 16 | hit | hit | hit | hit | hit | hit | hit | hit | hit | hit |
| soft 17 | hit | hit | hit | hit | hit | hit | hit | hit | hit | hit |
| soft 18 | st | st | st | st | st | st | st | hit | hit | hit |
| soft 19,20 | st | st | st | st | st | st | st | st | st | st |

| Pairs | | | | Dealer's Up Card | | | | | | |
|---|---|---|---|---|---|---|---|---|---|---|
| Your Hand | 2 | 3 | 4 | 5 | 6 | 7 | 8 | 9 | 10 | A |
| 2,2 | hit | hit | sp | sp | sp | sp | hit | hit | hit | hit |
| 3,3 | hit | hit | sp | sp | sp | sp | hit | hit | hit | hit |
| 4,4 | hit | hit | hit | hit | hit | hit | hit | hit | hit | hit |
| 5,5 | dd | dd | dd | dd | dd | dd | dd | dd | hit | hit |
| 6,6 | hit | sp | sp | sp | sp | hit | hit | hit | hit | hit |
| 7,7 | sp | sp | sp | sp | sp | sp | hit | hit | sur | sur |
| 8,8 | sp | sp | sp | sp | sp | sp | sp | sp | sur& | sur& |
| 9,9 | sp | sp | sp | sp | sp | st | sp | sp | st | st |
| 10,10 | st | st | st | st | st | st | st | st | st | st |
| A,A | sp | sp | sp | sp | sp | sp | sp | sp | sp | sp |

## CHART 21

Four decks

Dealer stands on soft 17

Double down on any hand

Doubling down after splitting is allowed

| Hard count | | | | Dealer's Up Card | | | | | | |
|---|---|---|---|---|---|---|---|---|---|---|
| Your Hand | 2 | 3 | 4 | 5 | 6 | 7 | 8 | 9 | 10 | A |
| 5 | hit | hit | hit | hit | hit | hit | hit | hit | hit | hit |
| 6 | hit | hit | hit | hit | hit | hit | hit | hit | hit | hit |
| 7 | hit | hit | hit | hit | hit | hit | hit | hit | hit | hit |
| 8 | hit | hit | hit | hit | hit | hit | hit | hit | hit | hit |
| 9 | hit | dd | dd | dd | dd | hit | hit | hit | hit | hit |
| 10 | dd | dd | dd | dd | dd | dd | dd | dd | hit | hit |
| 11 | dd | dd | dd | dd | dd | dd | dd | dd | dd | hit |
| 12 | hit | hit | st | st | st | hit | hit | hit | hit | hit |
| 13 | st | st | st | st | st | hit | hit | hit | hit | sur |

| | | | | | | | | | | |
|---|---|---|---|---|---|---|---|---|---|---|
| 14 | st | st | st | st | st | hit | hit | hit | sur | sur |
| 15 | st | st | st | st | st | hit | hit | hit | sur | sur |
| 16 | st | st | st | st | st | hit | hit | sur | sur | sur |
| 17–21 | st | st | st | st | st | st | st | st | st | st |

**Soft Count**                      **Dealer's Up Card**

| Your Hand | 2 | 3 | 4 | 5 | 6 | 7 | 8 | 9 | 10 | A |
|---|---|---|---|---|---|---|---|---|---|---|
| soft 13 | hit | hit | hit | dd | dd | hit | hit | hit | hit | hit |
| soft 14 | hit | hit | hit | dd | dd | hit | hit | hit | hit | hit |
| soft 15 | hit | hit | dd | dd | dd | hit | hit | hit | hit | hit |
| soft 16 | hit | hit | dd | dd | dd | hit | hit | hit | hit | hit |
| soft 17 | hit | dd | dd | dd | dd | hit | hit | hit | hit | hit |
| soft 18 | st | dd | dd | dd | dd | st | st | hit | hit | hit |
| soft 19,20 | st | st | st | st | st | st | st | st | st | st |

**Pairs**                               **Dealer's Up Card**

| Your Hand | 2 | 3 | 4 | 5 | 6 | 7 | 8 | 9 | 10 | A |
|---|---|---|---|---|---|---|---|---|---|---|
| 2,2 | sp | sp | sp | sp | sp | sp | hit | hit | hit | hit |
| 3,3 | sp | sp | sp | sp | sp | sp | hit | hit | hit | hit |
| 4,4 | hit | hit | hit | sp | sp | hit | hit | hit | hit | hit |
| 5,5 | dd | dd | dd | dd | dd | dd | dd | dd | hit | hit |
| 6,6 | sp | sp | sp | sp | sp | hit | hit | hit | hit | hit |
| 7,7 | sp | sp | sp | sp | sp | sp | hit | hit | sur | sur |
| 8,8 | sp | sp | sp | sp | sp | sp | sp | sp | sur& | sur& |
| 9,9 | sp | sp | sp | sp | sp | st | sp | sp | st | st |
| 10,10 | st | st | st | st | st | st | st | st | st | st |
| A,A | sp | sp | sp | sp | sp | sp | sp | sp | sp | sp |

# CHART 22

Four decks

Dealer stands on soft 17

Double down on any hand

No doubling down after splitting

| **Hard count** | | | | **Dealer's Up Card** | | | | | | |
|---|---|---|---|---|---|---|---|---|---|---|
| Your Hand | 2 | 3 | 4 | 5 | 6 | 7 | 8 | 9 | 10 | A |
| 5 | hit | hit | hit | hit | hit | hit | hit | hit | hit | hit |
| 6 | hit | hit | hit | hit | hit | hit | hit | hit | hit | hit |
| 7 | hit | hit | hit | hit | hit | hit | hit | hit | hit | hit |
| 8 | hit | hit | hit | hit | hit | hit | hit | hit | hit | hit |
| 9 | hit | dd | dd | dd | dd | hit | hit | hit | hit | hit |
| 10 | dd | dd | dd | dd | dd | dd | dd | dd | hit | hit |
| 11 | dd | dd | dd | dd | dd | dd | dd | dd | dd | hit |
| 12 | hit | hit | st | st | st | hit | hit | hit | hit | hit |
| 13 | st | st | st | st | st | hit | hit | hit | hit | sur |
| 14 | st | st | st | st | st | hit | hit | hit | sur | sur |
| 15 | st | st | st | st | st | hit | hit | hit | sur | sur |
| 16 | st | st | st | st | st | hit | hit | sur | sur | sur |
| 17–21 | st | st | st | st | st | st | st | st | st | st |

| **Soft Count** | | | | **Dealer's Up Card** | | | | | | |
|---|---|---|---|---|---|---|---|---|---|---|
| Your Hand | 2 | 3 | 4 | 5 | 6 | 7 | 8 | 9 | 10 | A |
| soft 13 | hit | hit | hit | dd | dd | hit | hit | hit | hit | hit |
| soft 14 | hit | hit | hit | dd | dd | hit | hit | hit | hit | hit |
| soft 15 | hit | hit | dd | dd | dd | hit | hit | hit | hit | hit |
| soft 16 | hit | hit | dd | dd | dd | hit | hit | hit | hit | hit |
| soft 17 | hit | dd | dd | dd | dd | hit | hit | hit | hit | hit |
| soft 18 | st | dd | dd | dd | dd | st | st | hit | hit | hit |
| soft 19,20 | st | st | st | st | st | st | st | st | st | st |

| Pairs | | | | Dealer's Up Card | | | | | | |
|---|---|---|---|---|---|---|---|---|---|---|
| Your Hand | 2 | 3 | 4 | 5 | 6 | 7 | 8 | 9 | 10 | A |
| 2,2 | hit | hit | sp | sp | sp | sp | hit | hit | hit | hit |
| 3,3 | hit | hit | sp | sp | sp | sp | hit | hit | hit | hit |
| 4,4 | hit | hit | hit | hit | hit | hit | hit | hit | hit | hit |
| 5,5 | dd | dd | dd | dd | dd | dd | dd | dd | hit | hit |
| 6,6 | hit | sp | sp | sp | sp | hit | hit | hit | hit | hit |
| 7,7 | sp | sp | sp | sp | sp | sp | hit | hit | sur | sur |
| 8,8 | sp | sp | sp | sp | sp | sp | sp | sp | sur& | sur& |
| 9,9 | sp | sp | sp | sp | sp | st | sp | sp | st | st |
| 10,10 | st | st | st | st | st | st | st | st | st | st |
| A,A | sp | sp | sp | sp | sp | sp | sp | sp | sp | sp |

## CHART 23

Four decks

Dealer stands on soft 17

Double down on 10 and 11 only

Doubling down after splitting is allowed

| Hard count | | | | Dealer's Up Card | | | | | | |
|---|---|---|---|---|---|---|---|---|---|---|
| Your Hand | 2 | 3 | 4 | 5 | 6 | 7 | 8 | 9 | 10 | A |
| 5 | hit | hit | hit | hit | hit | hit | hit | hit | hit | hit |
| 6 | hit | hit | hit | hit | hit | hit | hit | hit | hit | hit |
| 7 | hit | hit | hit | hit | hit | hit | hit | hit | hit | hit |
| 8 | hit | hit | hit | hit | hit | hit | hit | hit | hit | hit |
| 9 | hit | hit | hit | hit | hit | hit | hit | hit | hit | hit |
| 10 | dd | dd | dd | dd | dd | dd | dd | dd | hit | hit |
| 11 | dd | dd | dd | dd | dd | dd | dd | dd | dd | hit |
| 12 | hit | hit | st | st | st | hit | hit | hit | hit | hit |
| 13 | st | st | st | st | st | hit | hit | hit | hit | sur |
| 14 | st | st | st | st | st | hit | hit | hit | sur | sur |

| | | | | | | | | | | |
|---|---|---|---|---|---|---|---|---|---|---|
| 15 | st | st | st | st | st | hit | hit | hit | sur | sur |
| 16 | st | st | st | st | st | hit | hit | sur | sur | sur |
| 17–21 | st | st | st | st | st | st | st | st | st | st |

### Soft Count — Dealer's Up Card

| Your Hand | 2 | 3 | 4 | 5 | 6 | 7 | 8 | 9 | 10 | A |
|---|---|---|---|---|---|---|---|---|---|---|
| soft 13 | hit | hit | hit | hit | hit | hit | hit | hit | hit | hit |
| soft 14 | hit | hit | hit | hit | hit | hit | hit | hit | hit | hit |
| soft 15 | hit | hit | hit | hit | hit | hit | hit | hit | hit | hit |
| soft 16 | hit | hit | hit | hit | hit | hit | hit | hit | hit | hit |
| soft 17 | hit | hit | hit | hit | hit | hit | hit | hit | hit | hit |
| soft 18 | st | st | st | st | st | st | st | hit | hit | hit |
| soft 19,20 | st | st | st | st | st | st | st | st | st | st |

### Pairs — Dealer's Up Card

| Your Hand | 2 | 3 | 4 | 5 | 6 | 7 | 8 | 9 | 10 | A |
|---|---|---|---|---|---|---|---|---|---|---|
| 2,2 | sp | sp | sp | sp | sp | sp | hit | hit | hit | hit |
| 3,3 | sp | sp | sp | sp | sp | sp | hit | hit | hit | hit |
| 4,4 | hit | hit | hit | sp | sp | hit | hit | hit | hit | hit |
| 5,5 | dd | dd | dd | dd | dd | dd | dd | dd | hit | hit |
| 6,6 | sp | sp | sp | sp | sp | hit | hit | hit | hit | hit |
| 7,7 | sp | sp | sp | sp | sp | sp | hit | hit | sur | sur |
| 8,8 | sp | sp | sp | sp | sp | sp | sp | sp | sur& | sur& |
| 9,9 | sp | sp | sp | sp | sp | st | sp | sp | st | st |
| 10,10 | st | st | st | st | st | st | st | st | st | st |
| A,A | sp | sp | sp | sp | sp | sp | sp | sp | sp | sp |

# CHART 24

Four decks

Dealer stands on soft 17

Double down on 10 and 11 only

No doubling down after splitting

**Hard count**                          **Dealer's Up Card**

| Your Hand | 2 | 3 | 4 | 5 | 6 | 7 | 8 | 9 | 10 | A |
|-----------|-----|-----|-----|-----|-----|-----|-----|-----|-----|-----|
| 5 | hit | hit | hit | hit | hit | hit | hit | hit | hit | hit |
| 6 | hit | hit | hit | hit | hit | hit | hit | hit | hit | hit |
| 7 | hit | hit | hit | hit | hit | hit | hit | hit | hit | hit |
| 8 | hit | hit | hit | hit | hit | hit | hit | hit | hit | hit |
| 9 | hit | hit | hit | hit | hit | hit | hit | hit | hit | hit |
| 10 | dd | dd | dd | dd | dd | dd | dd | dd | hit | hit |
| 11 | dd | dd | dd | dd | dd | dd | dd | dd | dd | hit |
| 12 | hit | hit | st | st | st | hit | hit | hit | hit | hit |
| 13 | st | st | st | st | st | hit | hit | hit | hit | sur |
| 14 | st | st | st | st | st | hit | hit | hit | sur | sur |
| 15 | st | st | st | st | st | hit | hit | hit | sur | sur |
| 16 | st | st | st | st | st | hit | hit | sur | sur | sur |
| 17–21 | st | st | st | st | st | st | st | st | st | st |

**Soft Count**                          **Dealer's Up Card**

| Your Hand | 2 | 3 | 4 | 5 | 6 | 7 | 8 | 9 | 10 | A |
|-----------|-----|-----|-----|-----|-----|-----|-----|-----|-----|-----|
| soft 13 | hit | hit | hit | hit | hit | hit | hit | hit | hit | hit |
| soft 14 | hit | hit | hit | hit | hit | hit | hit | hit | hit | hit |
| soft 15 | hit | hit | hit | hit | hit | hit | hit | hit | hit | hit |
| soft 16 | hit | hit | hit | hit | hit | hit | hit | hit | hit | hit |
| soft 17 | hit | hit | hit | hit | hit | hit | hit | hit | hit | hit |
| soft 18 | st | st | st | st | st | st | st | hit | hit | hit |
| soft 19,20 | st | st | st | st | st | st | st | st | st | st |

| Pairs | Dealer's Up Card | | | | | | | | | |
|---|---|---|---|---|---|---|---|---|---|---|
| Your Hand | 2 | 3 | 4 | 5 | 6 | 7 | 8 | 9 | 10 | A |
| 2,2 | hit | hit | sp | sp | sp | sp | hit | hit | hit | hit |
| 3,3 | hit | hit | sp | sp | sp | sp | hit | hit | hit | hit |
| 4,4 | hit | hit | hit | hit | hit | hit | hit | hit | hit | hit |
| 5,5 | dd | dd | dd | dd | dd | dd | dd | dd | hit | hit |
| 6,6 | hit | sp | sp | sp | sp | hit | hit | hit | hit | hit |
| 7,7 | sp | sp | sp | sp | sp | sp | hit | hit | sur | sur |
| 8,8 | sp | sp | sp | sp | sp | sp | sp | sp | sur& | sur& |
| 9,9 | sp | sp | sp | sp | sp | st | sp | sp | st | st |
| 10,10 | st | st | st | st | st | st | st | st | st | st |
| A,A | sp | sp | sp | sp | sp | sp | sp | sp | sp | sp |

# CHART 25

Two decks

Dealer hits soft 17

Double down on any hand

Doubling down after splitting is allowed

| Hard count | Dealer's Up Card | | | | | | | | | |
|---|---|---|---|---|---|---|---|---|---|---|
| Your Hand | 2 | 3 | 4 | 5 | 6 | 7 | 8 | 9 | 10 | A |
| 5 | hit | hit | hit | hit | hit | hit | hit | hit | hit | hit |
| 6 | hit | hit | hit | hit | hit | hit | hit | hit | hit | hit |
| 7 | hit | hit | hit | hit | hit | hit | hit | hit | hit | hit |
| 8 | hit | hit | hit | hit | hit | hit | hit | hit | hit | hit |
| 9 | dd | dd | dd | dd | dd | hit | hit | hit | hit | hit |
| 10 | dd | dd | dd | dd | dd | dd | dd | dd | hit | hit |
| 11 | dd | dd | dd | dd | dd | dd | dd | dd | dd | dd |
| 12 | hit | hit | st | st | st | hit | hit | hit | hit | hit |
| 13 | st | st | st | st | st | hit | hit | hit | hit | sur |

| 14 | st | st | st | st | st | hit | hit | hit | sur | sur |
| 15 | st | st | st | st | st | hit | hit | hit | sur | sur |
| 16 | st | st | st | st | st | hit | hit | sur | sur | sur |
| 17–21 | st | st | st | st | st | st | st | st | st | st |

## Soft Count

| Your Hand | \#Dealer's Up Card | | | | | | | | | |
|---|---|---|---|---|---|---|---|---|---|---|
| | 2 | 3 | 4 | 5 | 6 | 7 | 8 | 9 | 10 | A |
| soft 13 | hit | hit | hit | dd | dd | hit | hit | hit | hit | hit |
| soft 14 | hit | hit | dd | dd | dd | hit | hit | hit | hit | hit |
| soft 15 | hit | hit | dd | dd | dd | hit | hit | hit | hit | hit |
| soft 16 | hit | hit | dd | dd | dd | hit | hit | hit | hit | hit |
| soft 17 | hit | dd | dd | dd | dd | hit | hit | hit | hit | hit |
| soft 18 | dd | dd | dd | dd | dd | st | st | hit | hit | hit |
| soft 19,20 | st | st | st | st | st | st | st | st | st | st |

## Pairs

| Your Hand | \#Dealer's Up Card | | | | | | | | | |
|---|---|---|---|---|---|---|---|---|---|---|
| | 2 | 3 | 4 | 5 | 6 | 7 | 8 | 9 | 10 | A |
| 2,2 | sp | sp | sp | sp | sp | sp | hit | hit | hit | hit |
| 3,3 | sp | sp | sp | sp | sp | sp | hit | hit | hit | hit |
| 4,4 | hit | hit | hit | sp | sp | hit | hit | hit | hit | hit |
| 5,5 | dd | dd | dd | dd | dd | dd | dd | dd | hit | hit |
| 6,6 | sp | sp | sp | sp | sp | sp | hit | hit | hit | hit |
| 7,7 | sp | sp | sp | sp | sp | sp | sp | hit | sur | sur |
| 8,8 | sp | sp | sp | sp | sp | sp | sp | sp | sur& | sur& |
| 9,9 | sp | sp | sp | sp | sp | st | sp | sp | st | st |
| 10,10 | st | st | st | st | st | st | st | st | st | st |
| A,A | sp | sp | sp | sp | sp | sp | sp | sp | sp | sp |

# CHART 26

Two decks

Dealer hits soft 17

Double down on any hand

No doubling down after splitting

**Hard count**                          **Dealer's Up Card**

| Your Hand | 2 | 3 | 4 | 5 | 6 | 7 | 8 | 9 | 10 | A |
|---|---|---|---|---|---|---|---|---|---|---|
| 5 | hit | hit | hit | hit | hit | hit | hit | hit | hit | hit |
| 6 | hit | hit | hit | hit | hit | hit | hit | hit | hit | hit |
| 7 | hit | hit | hit | hit | hit | hit | hit | hit | hit | hit |
| 8 | hit | hit | hit | hit | hit | hit | hit | hit | hit | hit |
| 9 | dd | dd | dd | dd | dd | hit | hit | hit | hit | hit |
| 10 | dd | dd | dd | dd | dd | dd | dd | dd | hit | hit |
| 11 | dd | dd | dd | dd | dd | dd | dd | dd | dd | dd |
| 12 | hit | hit | st | st | st | hit | hit | hit | hit | hit |
| 13 | st | st | st | st | st | hit | hit | hit | hit | sur |
| 14 | st | st | st | st | st | hit | hit | hit | sur | sur |
| 15 | st | st | st | st | st | hit | hit | hit | sur | sur |
| 16 | st | st | st | st | st | hit | hit | sur | sur | sur |
| 17–21 | st | st | st | st | st | st | st | st | st | st |

**Soft Count**                        **Dealer's Up Card**

| Your Hand | 2 | 3 | 4 | 5 | 6 | 7 | 8 | 9 | 10 | A |
|---|---|---|---|---|---|---|---|---|---|---|
| soft 13 | hit | hit | hit | dd | dd | hit | hit | hit | hit | hit |
| soft 14 | hit | hit | dd | dd | dd | hit | hit | hit | hit | hit |
| soft 15 | hit | hit | dd | dd | dd | hit | hit | hit | hit | hit |
| soft 16 | hit | hit | dd | dd | dd | hit | hit | hit | hit | hit |
| soft 17 | hit | dd | dd | dd | dd | hit | hit | hit | hit | hit |
| soft 18 | dd | dd | dd | dd | dd | st | st | hit | hit | hit |
| soft 19,20 | st | st | st | st | st | st | st | st | st | st |

| Pairs | Dealer's Up Card | | | | | | | | | |
|---|---|---|---|---|---|---|---|---|---|---|
| Your Hand | 2 | 3 | 4 | 5 | 6 | 7 | 8 | 9 | 10 | A |
| 2,2 | hit | hit | sp | sp | sp | sp | hit | hit | hit | hit |
| 3,3 | hit | hit | sp | sp | sp | sp | hit | hit | hit | hit |
| 4,4 | hit | hit | hit | hit | hit | hit | hit | hit | hit | hit |
| 5,5 | dd | dd | dd | dd | dd | dd | dd | dd | hit | hit |
| 6,6 | sp | sp | sp | sp | sp | hit | hit | hit | hit | hit |
| 7,7 | sp | sp | sp | sp | sp | sp | hit | hit | sur | sur |
| 8,8 | sp | sp | sp | sp | sp | sp | sp | sp | sur& | sur& |
| 9,9 | sp | sp | sp | sp | sp | st | sp | sp | st | st |
| 10,10 | st | st | st | st | st | st | st | st | st | st |
| A,A | sp | sp | sp | sp | sp | sp | sp | sp | sp | sp |

## CHART 27

Two decks

Dealer hits soft 17

Double down on 10 or 11 only

Doubling down after splitting is allowed

| Hard count | Dealer's Up Card | | | | | | | | | |
|---|---|---|---|---|---|---|---|---|---|---|
| Your Hand | 2 | 3 | 4 | 5 | 6 | 7 | 8 | 9 | 10 | A |
| 5 | hit | hit | hit | hit | hit | hit | hit | hit | hit | hit |
| 6 | hit | hit | hit | hit | hit | hit | hit | hit | hit | hit |
| 7 | hit | hit | hit | hit | hit | hit | hit | hit | hit | hit |
| 8 | hit | hit | hit | hit | hit | hit | hit | hit | hit | hit |
| 9 | hit | hit | hit | hit | hit | hit | hit | hit | hit | hit |
| 10 | dd | dd | dd | dd | dd | dd | dd | dd | hit | hit |
| 11 | dd | dd | dd | dd | dd | dd | dd | dd | dd | dd |
| 12 | hit | hit | st | st | st | hit | hit | hit | hit | hit |
| 13 | st | st | st | st | st | hit | hit | hit | hit | sur |
| 14 | st | st | st | st | st | hit | hit | hit | sur | sur |

| 15 | st | st | st | st | st | hit | hit | hit | sur | sur |
| 16 | st | st | st | st | st | hit | hit | sur | sur | sur |
| 17–21 | st | st | st | st | st | st | st | st | st | st |

### Soft Count — Dealer's Up Card

| Your Hand | 2 | 3 | 4 | 5 | 6 | 7 | 8 | 9 | 10 | A |
| --- | --- | --- | --- | --- | --- | --- | --- | --- | --- | --- |
| soft 13 | hit | hit | hit | hit | hit | hit | hit | hit | hit | hit |
| soft 14 | hit | hit | hit | hit | hit | hit | hit | hit | hit | hit |
| soft 15 | hit | hit | hit | hit | hit | hit | hit | hit | hit | hit |
| soft 16 | hit | hit | hit | hit | hit | hit | hit | hit | hit | hit |
| soft 17 | hit | hit | hit | hit | hit | hit | hit | hit | hit | hit |
| soft 18 | st | st | st | st | st | st | st | hit | hit | hit |
| soft 19,20 | st | st | st | st | st | st | st | st | st | st |

### Pairs — Dealer's Up Card

| Your Hand | 2 | 3 | 4 | 5 | 6 | 7 | 8 | 9 | 10 | A |
| --- | --- | --- | --- | --- | --- | --- | --- | --- | --- | --- |
| 2,2 | sp | sp | sp | sp | sp | sp | hit | hit | hit | hit |
| 3,3 | sp | sp | sp | sp | sp | sp | hit | hit | hit | hit |
| 4,4 | hit | hit | hit | sp | sp | hit | hit | hit | hit | hit |
| 5,5 | dd | dd | dd | dd | dd | dd | dd | dd | hit | hit |
| 6,6 | sp | sp | sp | sp | sp | sp | hit | hit | hit | hit |
| 7,7 | sp | sp | sp | sp | sp | sp | sp | hit | sur | sur |
| 8,8 | sp | sp | sp | sp | sp | sp | sp | sp | sur& | sur& |
| 9,9 | sp | sp | sp | sp | sp | st | sp | sp | st | st |
| 10,10 | st | st | st | st | st | st | st | st | st | st |
| A,A | sp | sp | sp | sp | sp | sp | sp | sp | sp | sp |

# CHART 28

Two decks

Dealer hits soft 17

Double down on 10 or 11 only

No doubling down after splitting

| **Hard count** | **Dealer's Up Card** | | | | | | | | | |
|---|---|---|---|---|---|---|---|---|---|---|
| Your Hand | 2 | 3 | 4 | 5 | 6 | 7 | 8 | 9 | 10 | A |
| 5 | hit | hit | hit | hit | hit | hit | hit | hit | hit | hit |
| 6 | hit | hit | hit | hit | hit | hit | hit | hit | hit | hit |
| 7 | hit | hit | hit | hit | hit | hit | hit | hit | hit | hit |
| 8 | hit | hit | hit | hit | hit | hit | hit | hit | hit | hit |
| 9 | hit | hit | hit | hit | hit | hit | hit | hit | hit | hit |
| 10 | dd | dd | dd | dd | dd | dd | dd | dd | hit | hit |
| 11 | dd | dd | dd | dd | dd | dd | dd | dd | dd | dd |
| 12 | hit | hit | st | st | st | hit | hit | hit | hit | hit |
| 13 | st | st | st | st | st | hit | hit | hit | hit | sur |
| 14 | st | st | st | st | st | hit | hit | hit | hit | sur |
| 15 | st | st | st | st | st | hit | hit | hit | sur | sur |
| 16 | st | st | st | st | st | hit | hit | sur | sur | sur |
| 17–21 | st | st | st | st | st | st | st | st | st | st |

| **Soft Count** | **Dealer's Up Card** | | | | | | | | | |
|---|---|---|---|---|---|---|---|---|---|---|
| Your Hand | 2 | 3 | 4 | 5 | 6 | 7 | 8 | 9 | 10 | A |
| soft 13 | hit | hit | hit | hit | hit | hit | hit | hit | hit | hit |
| soft 14 | hit | hit | hit | hit | hit | hit | hit | hit | hit | hit |
| soft 15 | hit | hit | hit | hit | hit | hit | hit | hit | hit | hit |
| soft 16 | hit | hit | hit | hit | hit | hit | hit | hit | hit | hit |
| soft 17 | hit | hit | hit | hit | hit | hit | hit | hit | hit | hit |
| soft 18 | st | st | st | st | st | st | st | hit | hit | hit |
| soft 19,20 | st | st | st | st | st | st | st | st | st | st |

**Pairs**                         **Dealer's Up Card**

| Your Hand | 2 | 3 | 4 | 5 | 6 | 7 | 8 | 9 | 10 | A |
|---|---|---|---|---|---|---|---|---|---|---|
| 2,2 | hit | hit | sp | sp | sp | sp | hit | hit | hit | hit |
| 3,3 | hit | hit | sp | sp | sp | sp | hit | hit | hit | hit |
| 4,4 | hit | hit | hit | hit | hit | hit | hit | hit | hit | hit |
| 5,5 | dd | dd | dd | dd | dd | dd | dd | dd | hit | hit |
| 6,6 | sp | sp | sp | sp | sp | hit | hit | hit | hit | hit |
| 7,7 | sp | sp | sp | sp | sp | sp | hit | hit | sur | sur |
| 8,8 | sp | sp | sp | sp | sp | sp | sp | sp | sur& | sur& |
| 9,9 | sp | sp | sp | sp | sp | st | sp | sp | st | st |
| 10,10 | st | st | st | st | st | st | st | st | st | st |
| A,A | sp | sp | sp | sp | sp | sp | sp | sp | sp | sp |

# CHART 29

Two decks

Dealer stands on soft 17

Double down on any hand

Doubling down after splitting is allowed

**Hard count**                     **Dealer's Up Card**

| Your Hand | 2 | 3 | 4 | 5 | 6 | 7 | 8 | 9 | 10 | A |
|---|---|---|---|---|---|---|---|---|---|---|
| 5 | hit | hit | hit | hit | hit | hit | hit | hit | hit | hit |
| 6 | hit | hit | hit | hit | hit | hit | hit | hit | hit | hit |
| 7 | hit | hit | hit | hit | hit | hit | hit | hit | hit | hit |
| 8 | hit | hit | hit | hit | hit | hit | hit | hit | hit | hit |
| 9 | dd | dd | dd | dd | dd | hit | hit | hit | hit | hit |
| 10 | dd | dd | dd | dd | dd | dd | dd | dd | hit | hit |
| 11 | dd | dd | dd | dd | dd | dd | dd | dd | dd | dd |
| 12 | hit | hit | st | st | st | hit | hit | hit | hit | hit |
| 13 | st | st | st | st | st | hit | hit | hit | hit | sur |

| | | | | | | | | | | |
|---|---|---|---|---|---|---|---|---|---|---|
| 14 | st | st | st | st | st | hit | hit | hit | sur | sur |
| 15 | st | st | st | st | st | hit | hit | hit | sur | sur |
| 16 | st | st | st | st | st | hit | hit | sur | sur | sur |
| 17–21 | st | st | st | st | st | st | st | st | st | st |

| Soft Count | Dealer's Up Card | | | | | | | | | |
|---|---|---|---|---|---|---|---|---|---|---|
| Your Hand | 2 | 3 | 4 | 5 | 6 | 7 | 8 | 9 | 10 | A |
| soft 13 | hit | hit | hit | dd | dd | hit | hit | hit | hit | hit |
| soft 14 | hit | hit | hit | dd | dd | hit | hit | hit | hit | hit |
| soft 15 | hit | hit | dd | dd | dd | hit | hit | hit | hit | hit |
| soft 16 | hit | hit | dd | dd | dd | hit | hit | hit | hit | hit |
| soft 17 | hit | dd | dd | dd | dd | hit | hit | hit | hit | hit |
| soft 18 | st | dd | dd | dd | dd | st | st | hit | hit | hit |
| soft 19,20 | st | st | st | st | st | st | st | st | st | st |

| Pairs | Dealer's Up Card | | | | | | | | | |
|---|---|---|---|---|---|---|---|---|---|---|
| Your Hand | 2 | 3 | 4 | 5 | 6 | 7 | 8 | 9 | 10 | A |
| 2,2 | sp | sp | sp | sp | sp | sp | hit | hit | hit | hit |
| 3,3 | sp | sp | sp | sp | sp | sp | hit | hit | hit | hit |
| 4,4 | hit | hit | hit | sp | sp | hit | hit | hit | hit | hit |
| 5,5 | dd | dd | dd | dd | dd | dd | dd | dd | hit | hit |
| 6,6 | sp | sp | sp | sp | sp | sp | hit | hit | hit | hit |
| 7,7 | sp | sp | sp | sp | sp | sp | sp | hit | sur | sur |
| 8,8 | sp | sp | sp | sp | sp | sp | sp | sp | sur& | sur& |
| 9,9 | sp | sp | sp | sp | sp | st | sp | sp | st | st |
| 10,10 | st | st | st | st | st | st | st | st | st | st |
| A,A | sp | sp | sp | sp | sp | sp | sp | sp | sp | sp |

## CHART 30

Two decks

Dealer stands on soft 17

Double down on any hand

No doubling down after splitting

| **Hard count** | | | | **Dealer's Up Card** | | | | | | |
|---|---|---|---|---|---|---|---|---|---|---|
| Your Hand | 2 | 3 | 4 | 5 | 6 | 7 | 8 | 9 | 10 | A |
| 5 | hit | hit | hit | hit | hit | hit | hit | hit | hit | hit |
| 6 | hit | hit | hit | hit | hit | hit | hit | hit | hit | hit |
| 7 | hit | hit | hit | hit | hit | hit | hit | hit | hit | hit |
| 8 | hit | hit | hit | hit | hit | hit | hit | hit | hit | hit |
| 9 | dd | dd | dd | dd | dd | hit | hit | hit | hit | hit |
| 10 | dd | dd | dd | dd | dd | dd | dd | dd | hit | hit |
| 11 | dd | dd | dd | dd | dd | dd | dd | dd | dd | dd |
| 12 | hit | hit | st | st | st | hit | hit | hit | hit | hit |
| 13 | st | st | st | st | st | hit | hit | hit | hit | sur |
| 14 | st | st | st | st | st | hit | hit | hit | sur | sur |
| 15 | st | st | st | st | st | hit | hit | hit | sur | sur |
| 16 | st | st | st | st | st | hit | hit | sur | sur | sur |
| 17–21 | st | st | st | st | st | st | st | st | st | st |

| **Soft Count** | | | | **Dealer's Up Card** | | | | | | |
|---|---|---|---|---|---|---|---|---|---|---|
| Your Hand | 2 | 3 | 4 | 5 | 6 | 7 | 8 | 9 | 10 | A |
| soft 13 | hit | hit | hit | dd | dd | hit | hit | hit | hit | hit |
| soft 14 | hit | hit | hit | dd | dd | hit | hit | hit | hit | hit |
| soft 15 | hit | hit | dd | dd | dd | hit | hit | hit | hit | hit |
| soft 16 | hit | hit | dd | dd | dd | hit | hit | hit | hit | hit |
| soft 17 | hit | dd | dd | dd | dd | hit | hit | hit | hit | hit |
| soft 18 | st | dd | dd | dd | dd | st | st | hit | hit | hit |
| soft 19,20 | st | st | st | st | st | st | st | st | st | st |

**Pairs**  **Dealer's Up Card**

| Your Hand | 2 | 3 | 4 | 5 | 6 | 7 | 8 | 9 | 10 | A |
|---|---|---|---|---|---|---|---|---|---|---|
| 2,2 | hit | hit | sp | sp | sp | sp | hit | hit | hit | hit |
| 3,3 | hit | hit | sp | sp | sp | sp | hit | hit | hit | hit |
| 4,4 | hit | hit | hit | hit | hit | hit | hit | hit | hit | hit |
| 5,5 | dd | dd | dd | dd | dd | dd | dd | dd | hit | hit |
| 6,6 | hit | sp | sp | sp | sp | hit | hit | hit | hit | hit |
| 7,7 | sp | sp | sp | sp | sp | sp | hit | hit | sur | sur |
| 8,8 | sp | sp | sp | sp | sp | sp | sp | sp | sur& | sur& |
| 9,9 | sp | sp | sp | sp | sp | st | sp | sp | st | st |
| 10,10 | st | st | st | st | st | st | st | st | st | st |
| A,A | sp | sp | sp | sp | sp | sp | sp | sp | sp | sp |

# CHART 31

Two decks

Dealer stands on soft 17

Double down on 10 and 11 only

Doubling down after splitting is allowed

**Hard count**  **Dealer's Up Card**

| Your Hand | 2 | 3 | 4 | 5 | 6 | 7 | 8 | 9 | 10 | A |
|---|---|---|---|---|---|---|---|---|---|---|
| 5 | hit | hit | hit | hit | hit | hit | hit | hit | hit | hit |
| 6 | hit | hit | hit | hit | hit | hit | hit | hit | hit | hit |
| 7 | hit | hit | hit | hit | hit | hit | hit | hit | hit | hit |
| 8 | hit | hit | hit | hit | hit | hit | hit | hit | hit | hit |
| 9 | hit | hit | hit | hit | hit | hit | hit | hit | hit | hit |
| 10 | dd | dd | dd | dd | dd | dd | dd | dd | hit | hit |
| 11 | dd | dd | dd | dd | dd | dd | dd | dd | dd | dd |
| 12 | hit | hit | st | st | st | hit | hit | hit | hit | hit |
| 13 | st | st | st | st | st | hit | hit | hit | hit | sur |

| | 2 | 3 | 4 | 5 | 6 | 7 | 8 | 9 | 10 | A |
|---|---|---|---|---|---|---|---|---|---|---|
| 14 | st | st | st | st | st | hit | hit | hit | sur | sur |
| 15 | st | st | st | st | st | hit | hit | hit | sur | sur |
| 16 | st | st | st | st | st | hit | hit | sur | sur | sur |
| 17–21 | st | st | st | st | st | st | st | st | st | st |

**Soft Count**　　　　　　　　**Dealer's Up Card**

| Your Hand | 2 | 3 | 4 | 5 | 6 | 7 | 8 | 9 | 10 | A |
|---|---|---|---|---|---|---|---|---|---|---|
| soft 13 | hit | hit | hit | hit | hit | hit | hit | hit | hit | hit |
| soft 14 | hit | hit | hit | hit | hit | hit | hit | hit | hit | hit |
| soft 15 | hit | hit | hit | hit | hit | hit | hit | hit | hit | hit |
| soft 16 | hit | hit | hit | hit | hit | hit | hit | hit | hit | hit |
| soft 17 | hit | hit | hit | hit | hit | hit | hit | hit | hit | hit |
| soft 18 | st | st | st | st | st | st | st | hit | hit | hit |
| soft 19,20 | st | st | st | st | st | st | st | st | st | st |

**Pairs**　　　　　　　　**Dealer's Up Card**

| Your Hand | 2 | 3 | 4 | 5 | 6 | 7 | 8 | 9 | 10 | A |
|---|---|---|---|---|---|---|---|---|---|---|
| 2,2 | sp | sp | sp | sp | sp | sp | hit | hit | hit | hit |
| 3,3 | sp | sp | sp | sp | sp | sp | hit | hit | hit | hit |
| 4,4 | hit | hit | hit | sp | sp | hit | hit | hit | hit | hit |
| 5,5 | dd | dd | dd | dd | dd | dd | dd | dd | hit | hit |
| 6,6 | sp | sp | sp | sp | sp | sp | hit | hit | hit | hit |
| 7,7 | sp | sp | sp | sp | sp | sp | sp | hit | sur | sur |
| 8,8 | sp | sp | sp | sp | sp | sp | sp | sp | sur& | sur& |
| 9,9 | sp | sp | sp | sp | sp | st | sp | sp | st | st |
| 10,10 | st | st | st | st | st | st | st | st | st | st |
| A,A | sp | sp | sp | sp | sp | sp | sp | sp | sp | sp |

# CHART 32

Two decks

Dealer stands on soft 17

Double down on 10 and 11 only

No doubling down after splitting

**Hard count**                             **Dealer's Up Card**

| Your Hand | 2 | 3 | 4 | 5 | 6 | 7 | 8 | 9 | 10 | A |
|---|---|---|---|---|---|---|---|---|---|---|
| 5 | hit | hit | hit | hit | hit | hit | hit | hit | hit | hit |
| 6 | hit | hit | hit | hit | hit | hit | hit | hit | hit | hit |
| 7 | hit | hit | hit | hit | hit | hit | hit | hit | hit | hit |
| 8 | hit | hit | hit | hit | hit | hit | hit | hit | hit | hit |
| 9 | hit | hit | hit | hit | hit | hit | hit | hit | hit | hit |
| 10 | dd | dd | dd | dd | dd | dd | dd | dd | hit | hit |
| 11 | dd | dd | dd | dd | dd | dd | dd | dd | dd | dd |
| 12 | hit | hit | st | st | st | hit | hit | hit | hit | hit |
| 13 | st | st | st | st | st | hit | hit | hit | hit | sur |
| 14 | st | st | st | st | st | hit | hit | hit | sur | sur |
| 15 | st | st | st | st | st | hit | hit | hit | sur | sur |
| 16 | st | st | st | st | st | hit | hit | sur | sur | sur |
| 17–21 | st | st | st | st | st | st | st | st | st | st |

**Soft Count**                             **Dealer's Up Card**

| Your Hand | 2 | 3 | 4 | 5 | 6 | 7 | 8 | 9 | 10 | A |
|---|---|---|---|---|---|---|---|---|---|---|
| soft 13 | hit | hit | hit | hit | hit | hit | hit | hit | hit | hit |
| soft 14 | hit | hit | hit | hit | hit | hit | hit | hit | hit | hit |
| soft 15 | hit | hit | hit | hit | hit | hit | hit | hit | hit | hit |
| soft 16 | hit | hit | hit | hit | hit | hit | hit | hit | hit | hit |
| soft 17 | hit | hit | hit | hit | hit | hit | hit | hit | hit | hit |
| soft 18 | st | st | st | st | st | st | st | hit | hit | hit |
| soft 19,20 | st | st | st | st | st | st | st | st | st | st |

| Pairs | | | | Dealer's Up Card | | | | | | |
|-------|---|---|---|---|---|---|---|---|---|---|
| Your Hand | 2 | 3 | 4 | 5 | 6 | 7 | 8 | 9 | 10 | A |
| 2,2 | hit | hit | sp | sp | sp | sp | hit | hit | hit | hit |
| 3,3 | hit | hit | sp | sp | sp | sp | hit | hit | hit | hit |
| 4,4 | hit | hit | hit | hit | hit | hit | hit | hit | hit | hit |
| 5,5 | dd | dd | dd | dd | dd | dd | dd | dd | hit | hit |
| 6,6 | hit | sp | sp | sp | sp | sp | hit | hit | hit | hit |
| 7,7 | sp | sp | sp | sp | sp | sp | hit | hit | sur | sur |
| 8,8 | sp | sp | sp | sp | sp | sp | sp | sp | sur& | sur& |
| 9,9 | sp | sp | sp | sp | sp | st | sp | sp | st | st |
| 10,10 | st | st | st | st | st | st | st | st | st | st |
| A,A | sp | sp | sp | sp | sp | sp | sp | sp | sp | sp |

# CHART 33

One deck

Dealer hits soft 17

Double down on any hand

Doubling down after splitting is allowed

| Hard count | | | | Dealer's Up Card | | | | | | |
|------------|---|---|---|---|---|---|---|---|---|---|
| Your Hand | 2 | 3 | 4 | 5 | 6 | 7 | 8 | 9 | 10 | A |
| 5 | hit | hit | hit | hit | hit | hit | hit | hit | hit | hit |
| 6 | hit | hit | hit | hit | hit | hit | hit | hit | hit | hit |
| 7 | hit | hit | hit | hit | hit | hit | hit | hit | hit | hit |
| 8 | hit | hit | hit | dd | dd | hit | hit | hit | hit | hit |
| 9 | dd | dd | dd | dd | dd | hit | hit | hit | hit | hit |
| 10 | dd | dd | dd | dd | dd | dd | dd | dd | hit | hit |
| 11 | dd | dd | dd | dd | dd | dd | dd | dd | dd | dd |
| 12 | hit | hit | st | st | st | hit | hit | hit | hit | hit |
| 13 | st | st | st | st | st | hit | hit | hit | hit | sur |

| | | | | | | | | | | |
|---|---|---|---|---|---|---|---|---|---|---|
| 14 | st | st | st | st | st | hit | hit | hit | sur | sur |
| 15 | st | st | st | st | st | hit | hit | hit | sur | sur |
| 16 | st | st | st | st | st | hit | hit | sur | sur | sur |
| 17–21 | st | st | st | st | st | st | st | st | st | st |

**Soft Count**                             **Dealer's Up Card**

| Your Hand | 2 | 3 | 4 | 5 | 6 | 7 | 8 | 9 | 10 | A |
|---|---|---|---|---|---|---|---|---|---|---|
| soft 13 | hit | hit | dd | dd | dd | hit | hit | hit | hit | hit |
| soft 14 | hit | hit | dd | dd | dd | hit | hit | hit | hit | hit |
| soft 15 | hit | hit | dd | dd | dd | hit | hit | hit | hit | hit |
| soft 16 | hit | hit | dd | dd | dd | hit | hit | hit | hit | hit |
| soft 17 | dd | dd | dd | dd | dd | hit | hit | hit | hit | hit |
| soft 18 | st | dd | dd | dd | dd | st | st | hit | hit | hit |
| soft 19,20 | st | st | st | st | st | st | st | st | st | st |

**Pairs**                                    **Dealer's Up Card**

| Your Hand | 2 | 3 | 4 | 5 | 6 | 7 | 8 | 9 | 10 | A |
|---|---|---|---|---|---|---|---|---|---|---|
| 2,2 | sp | sp | sp | sp | sp | sp | hit | hit | hit | hit |
| 3,3 | sp | sp | sp | sp | sp | sp | sp | hit | hit | hit |
| 4,4 | hit | hit | sp | sp | sp | hit | hit | hit | hit | hit |
| 5,5 | dd | dd | dd | dd | dd | dd | dd | dd | hit | hit |
| 6,6 | sp | sp | sp | sp | sp | sp | hit | hit | hit | hit |
| 7,7 | sp | sp | sp | sp | sp | sp | sp | hit | sur | sur |
| 8,8 | sp | sp | sp | sp | sp | sp | sp | sp | sur& | sur& |
| 9,9 | sp | sp | sp | sp | sp | st | sp | sp | st | st |
| 10,10 | st | st | st | st | st | st | st | st | st | st |
| A,A | sp | sp | sp | sp | sp | sp | sp | sp | sp | sp |

## CHART 34

One deck

Dealer hits soft 17

Double down on any hand

No doubling down after splitting

**Hard count**          **Dealer's Up Card**

| Your Hand | 2 | 3 | 4 | 5 | 6 | 7 | 8 | 9 | 10 | A |
|---|---|---|---|---|---|---|---|---|---|---|
| 5 | hit | hit | hit | hit | hit | hit | hit | hit | hit | hit |
| 6 | hit | hit | hit | hit | hit | hit | hit | hit | hit | hit |
| 7 | hit | hit | hit | hit | hit | hit | hit | hit | hit | hit |
| 8 | hit | hit | hit | dd | dd | hit | hit | hit | hit | hit |
| 9 | hit | dd | dd | dd | dd | hit | hit | hit | hit | hit |
| 10 | dd | dd | dd | dd | dd | dd | dd | dd | hit | hit |
| 11 | dd | dd | dd | dd | dd | dd | dd | dd | dd | dd |
| 12 | hit | hit | st | st | st | hit | hit | hit | hit | hit |
| 13 | st | st | st | st | st | hit | hit | hit | hit | sur |
| 14 | st | st | st | st | st | hit | hit | hit | sur | sur |
| 15 | st | st | st | st | st | hit | hit | hit | sur | sur |
| 16 | st | st | st | st | st | hit | hit | sur | sur | sur |
| 17–21 | st | st | st | st | st | st | st | st | st | st |

**Soft Count**          **Dealer's Up Card**

| Your Hand | 2 | 3 | 4 | 5 | 6 | 7 | 8 | 9 | 10 | A |
|---|---|---|---|---|---|---|---|---|---|---|
| soft 13 | hit | hit | dd | dd | dd | hit | hit | hit | hit | hit |
| soft 14 | hit | hit | dd | dd | dd | hit | hit | hit | hit | hit |
| soft 15 | hit | hit | dd | dd | dd | hit | hit | hit | hit | hit |
| soft 16 | hit | hit | dd | dd | dd | hit | hit | hit | hit | hit |
| soft 17 | dd | dd | dd | dd | dd | hit | hit | hit | hit | hit |
| soft 18 | st | dd | dd | dd | dd | st | st | hit | hit | hit |
| soft 19,20 | st | st | st | st | st | st | st | st | st | st |

**Pairs**                     **Dealer's Up Card**

| Your Hand | 2 | 3 | 4 | 5 | 6 | 7 | 8 | 9 | 10 | A |
|---|---|---|---|---|---|---|---|---|---|---|
| 2,2 | hit | sp | sp | sp | sp | sp | hit | hit | hit | hit |
| 3,3 | hit | hit | sp | sp | sp | sp | hit | hit | hit | hit |
| 4,4 | hit | hit | hit | dd | dd | hit | hit | hit | hit | hit |
| 5,5 | dd | dd | dd | dd | dd | dd | dd | dd | hit | hit |
| 6,6 | sp | sp | sp | sp | sp | hit | hit | hit | hit | hit |
| 7,7 | sp | sp | sp | sp | sp | sp | hit | hit | sur | sur |
| 8,8 | sp | sp | sp | sp | sp | sp | sp | sp | sur& | sur& |
| 9,9 | sp | sp | sp | sp | sp | st | sp | sp | st | st |
| 10,10 | st | st | st | st | st | st | st | st | st | st |
| A,A | sp | sp | sp | sp | sp | sp | sp | sp | sp | sp |

# CHART 35

One deck

Dealer hits soft 17

Double down on 10 or 11 only

Doubling down after splitting is allowed

**Hard count**                **Dealer's Up Card**

| Your Hand | 2 | 3 | 4 | 5 | 6 | 7 | 8 | 9 | 10 | A |
|---|---|---|---|---|---|---|---|---|---|---|
| 5 | hit | hit | hit | hit | hit | hit | hit | hit | hit | hit |
| 6 | hit | hit | hit | hit | hit | hit | hit | hit | hit | hit |
| 7 | hit | hit | hit | hit | hit | hit | hit | hit | hit | hit |
| 8 | hit | hit | hit | hit | hit | hit | hit | hit | hit | hit |
| 9 | hit | hit | hit | hit | hit | hit | hit | hit | hit | hit |
| 10 | dd | dd | dd | dd | dd | dd | dd | dd | hit | hit |
| 11 | dd | dd | dd | dd | dd | dd | dd | dd | dd | dd |
| 12 | hit | hit | st | st | st | hit | hit | hit | hit | hit |
| 13 | st | st | st | st | st | hit | hit | hit | hit | sur |

| 14 | st | st | st | st | st | hit | hit | hit | sur | sur |
|---|---|---|---|---|---|---|---|---|---|---|
| 15 | st | st | st | st | st | hit | hit | hit | sur | sur |
| 16 | st | st | st | st | st | hit | hit | sur | sur | sur |
| 17–21 | st | st | st | st | st | st | st | st | st | st |

### Soft Count — Dealer's Up Card

| Your Hand | 2 | 3 | 4 | 5 | 6 | 7 | 8 | 9 | 10 | A |
|---|---|---|---|---|---|---|---|---|---|---|
| soft 13 | hit | hit | hit | hit | hit | hit | hit | hit | hit | hit |
| soft 14 | hit | hit | hit | hit | hit | hit | hit | hit | hit | hit |
| soft 15 | hit | hit | hit | hit | hit | hit | hit | hit | hit | hit |
| soft 16 | hit | hit | hit | hit | hit | hit | hit | hit | hit | hit |
| soft 17 | hit | hit | hit | hit | hit | hit | hit | hit | hit | hit |
| soft 18 | st | st | st | st | st | st | st | hit | hit | hit |
| soft 19,20 | st | st | st | st | st | st | st | st | st | st |

### Pairs — Dealer's Up Card

| Your Hand | 2 | 3 | 4 | 5 | 6 | 7 | 8 | 9 | 10 | A |
|---|---|---|---|---|---|---|---|---|---|---|
| 2,2 | sp | sp | sp | sp | sp | sp | hit | hit | hit | hit |
| 3,3 | sp | sp | sp | sp | sp | sp | sp | hit | hit | hit |
| 4,4 | hit | hit | sp | sp | sp | hit | hit | hit | hit | hit |
| 5,5 | dd | dd | dd | dd | dd | dd | dd | dd | hit | hit |
| 6,6 | sp | sp | sp | sp | sp | sp | hit | hit | hit | hit |
| 7,7 | sp | sp | sp | sp | sp | sp | sp | hit | sur | sur |
| 8,8 | sp | sp | sp | sp | sp | sp | sp | sp | sur& | sur& |
| 9,9 | sp | sp | sp | sp | sp | st | sp | sp | st | st |
| 10,10 | st | st | st | st | st | st | st | st | st | st |
| A,A | sp | sp | sp | sp | sp | sp | sp | sp | sp | sp |

# CHART 36

One deck

Dealer hits soft 17

Double down on 10 or 11 only

No doubling down after splitting

| Hard count | | | | Dealer's Up Card | | | | | | |
|---|---|---|---|---|---|---|---|---|---|---|
| Your Hand | 2 | 3 | 4 | 5 | 6 | 7 | 8 | 9 | 10 | A |
| 5 | hit | hit | hit | hit | hit | hit | hit | hit | hit | hit |
| 6 | hit | hit | hit | hit | hit | hit | hit | hit | hit | hit |
| 7 | hit | hit | hit | hit | hit | hit | hit | hit | hit | hit |
| 8 | hit | hit | hit | hit | hit | hit | hit | hit | hit | hit |
| 9 | hit | hit | hit | hit | hit | hit | hit | hit | hit | hit |
| 10 | dd | dd | dd | dd | dd | dd | dd | dd | hit | hit |
| 11 | dd | dd | dd | dd | dd | dd | dd | dd | dd | dd |
| 12 | hit | hit | st | st | st | hit | hit | hit | hit | hit |
| 13 | st | st | st | st | st | hit | hit | hit | hit | sur |
| 14 | st | st | st | st | st | hit | hit | hit | sur | sur |
| 15 | st | st | st | st | st | hit | hit | hit | sur | sur |
| 16 | st | st | st | st | st | hit | hit | sur | sur | sur |
| 17–21 | st | st | st | st | st | st | st | st | st | st |

| Soft Count | | | | Dealer's Up Card | | | | | | |
|---|---|---|---|---|---|---|---|---|---|---|
| Your Hand | 2 | 3 | 4 | 5 | 6 | 7 | 8 | 9 | 10 | A |
| soft 13 | hit | hit | hit | hit | hit | hit | hit | hit | hit | hit |
| soft 14 | hit | hit | hit | hit | hit | hit | hit | hit | hit | hit |
| soft 15 | hit | hit | hit | hit | hit | hit | hit | hit | hit | hit |
| soft 16 | hit | hit | hit | hit | hit | hit | hit | hit | hit | hit |
| soft 17 | hit | hit | hit | hit | hit | hit | hit | hit | hit | hit |
| soft 18 | st | st | st | st | st | st | st | hit | hit | hit |
| soft 19,20 | st | st | st | st | st | st | st | st | st | st |

**Pairs** **Dealer's Up Card**

| Your Hand | 2 | 3 | 4 | 5 | 6 | 7 | 8 | 9 | 10 | A |
|---|---|---|---|---|---|---|---|---|---|---|
| 2,2 | hit | sp | sp | sp | sp | sp | hit | hit | hit | hit |
| 3,3 | hit | hit | sp | sp | sp | sp | hit | hit | hit | hit |
| 4,4 | hit | hit | hit | dd | dd | hit | hit | hit | hit | hit |
| 5,5 | dd | dd | dd | dd | dd | dd | dd | dd | hit | hit |
| 6,6 | sp | sp | sp | sp | sp | hit | hit | hit | hit | hit |
| 7,7 | sp | sp | sp | sp | sp | sp | hit | hit | sur | sur |
| 8,8 | sp | sp | sp | sp | sp | sp | sp | sp | sur& | sur& |
| 9,9 | sp | sp | sp | sp | sp | st | sp | sp | st | st |
| 10,10 | st | st | st | st | st | st | st | st | st | st |
| A,A | sp | sp | sp | sp | sp | sp | sp | sp | sp | sp |

# CHART 37

One deck

Dealer stands on soft 17

Double down on any hand

Doubling down after splitting is allowed

**Hard count** **Dealer's Up Card**

| Your Hand | 2 | 3 | 4 | 5 | 6 | 7 | 8 | 9 | 10 | A |
|---|---|---|---|---|---|---|---|---|---|---|
| 5 | hit | hit | hit | hit | hit | hit | hit | hit | hit | hit |
| 6 | hit | hit | hit | hit | hit | hit | hit | hit | hit | hit |
| 7 | hit | hit | hit | hit | hit | hit | hit | hit | hit | hit |
| 8 | hit | hit | hit | dd | dd | hit | hit | hit | hit | hit |
| 9 | dd | dd | dd | dd | dd | hit | hit | hit | hit | hit |
| 10 | dd | dd | dd | dd | dd | dd | dd | dd | hit | hit |
| 11 | dd | dd | dd | dd | dd | dd | dd | dd | dd | dd |
| 12 | hit | hit | st | st | st | hit | hit | hit | hit | hit |
| 13 | st | st | st | st | st | hit | hit | hit | hit | sur |

| | | | | | | | | | | |
|---|---|---|---|---|---|---|---|---|---|---|
| 14 | st | st | st | st | st | hit | hit | hit | sur | sur |
| 15 | st | st | st | st | st | hit | hit | hit | sur | sur |
| 16 | st | st | st | st | st | hit | hit | sur | sur | sur |
| 17–21 | st | st | st | st | st | st | st | st | st | st |

## Soft Count       Dealer's Up Card

| Your Hand | 2 | 3 | 4 | 5 | 6 | 7 | 8 | 9 | 10 | A |
|---|---|---|---|---|---|---|---|---|---|---|
| soft 13 | hit | hit | dd | dd | dd | hit | hit | hit | hit | hit |
| soft 14 | hit | hit | dd | dd | dd | hit | hit | hit | hit | hit |
| soft 15 | hit | hit | dd | dd | dd | hit | hit | hit | hit | hit |
| soft 16 | hit | hit | dd | dd | dd | hit | hit | hit | hit | hit |
| soft 17 | dd | dd | dd | dd | dd | hit | hit | hit | hit | hit |
| soft 18 | st | dd | dd | dd | dd | st | st | hit | hit | st |
| soft 19,20 | st | st | st | st | st | st | st | st | st | st |

## Pairs       Dealer's Up Card

| Your Hand | 2 | 3 | 4 | 5 | 6 | 7 | 8 | 9 | 10 | A |
|---|---|---|---|---|---|---|---|---|---|---|
| 2,2 | sp | sp | sp | sp | sp | sp | hit | hit | hit | hit |
| 3,3 | sp | sp | sp | sp | sp | sp | sp | hit | hit | hit |
| 4,4 | hit | hit | sp | sp | sp | hit | hit | hit | hit | hit |
| 5,5 | dd | dd | dd | dd | dd | dd | dd | dd | hit | hit |
| 6,6 | sp | sp | sp | sp | sp | sp | hit | hit | hit | hit |
| 7,7 | sp | sp | sp | sp | sp | sp | sp | hit | sur | sur |
| 8,8 | sp | sp | sp | sp | sp | sp | sp | sp | sur& | sur& |
| 9,9 | sp | sp | sp | sp | sp | st | sp | sp | st | st |
| 10,10 | st | st | st | st | st | st | st | st | st | st |
| A,A | sp | sp | sp | sp | sp | sp | sp | sp | sp | sp |

# CHART 38

One deck

Dealer stands on soft 17

Double down on any hand

No doubling down after splitting

| **Hard count** | | | | **Dealer's Up Card** | | | | | | |
|---|---|---|---|---|---|---|---|---|---|---|
| Your Hand | 2 | 3 | 4 | 5 | 6 | 7 | 8 | 9 | 10 | A |
| 5 | hit | hit | hit | hit | hit | hit | hit | hit | hit | hit |
| 6 | hit | hit | hit | hit | hit | hit | hit | hit | hit | hit |
| 7 | hit | hit | hit | hit | hit | hit | hit | hit | hit | hit |
| 8 | hit | hit | hit | dd | dd | hit | hit | hit | hit | hit |
| 9 | hit | dd | dd | dd | dd | hit | hit | hit | hit | hit |
| 10 | dd | dd | dd | dd | dd | dd | dd | dd | hit | hit |
| 11 | dd | dd | dd | dd | dd | dd | dd | dd | dd | dd |
| 12 | hit | hit | st | st | st | hit | hit | hit | hit | hit |
| 13 | st | st | st | st | st | hit | hit | hit | hit | sur |
| 14 | st | st | st | st | st | hit | hit | hit | sur | sur |
| 15 | st | st | st | st | st | hit | hit | hit | sur | sur |
| 16 | st | st | st | st | st | hit | hit | sur | sur | sur |
| 17–21 | st | st | st | st | st | st | st | st | st | st |

| **Soft Count** | | | | **Dealer's Up Card** | | | | | | |
|---|---|---|---|---|---|---|---|---|---|---|
| Your Hand | 2 | 3 | 4 | 5 | 6 | 7 | 8 | 9 | 10 | A |
| soft 13 | hit | hit | dd | dd | dd | hit | hit | hit | hit | hit |
| soft 14 | hit | hit | dd | dd | dd | hit | hit | hit | hit | hit |
| soft 15 | hit | hit | dd | dd | dd | hit | hit | hit | hit | hit |
| soft 16 | hit | hit | dd | dd | dd | hit | hit | hit | hit | hit |
| soft 17 | dd | dd | dd | dd | dd | hit | hit | hit | hit | hit |
| soft 18 | st | dd | dd | dd | dd | st | st | hit | hit | st |
| soft 19,20 | st | st | st | st | st | st | st | st | st | st |

**Pairs** **Dealer's Up Card**

| Your Hand | 2 | 3 | 4 | 5 | 6 | 7 | 8 | 9 | 10 | A |
|---|---|---|---|---|---|---|---|---|---|---|
| 2,2 | hit | sp | sp | sp | sp | sp | hit | hit | hit | hit |
| 3,3 | sp | sp | sp | sp | sp | sp | sp | hit | hit | hit |
| 4,4 | hit | hit | hit | dd | dd | hit | hit | hit | hit | hit |
| 5,5 | dd | dd | dd | dd | dd | dd | dd | dd | hit | hit |
| 6,6 | sp | sp | sp | sp | sp | hit | hit | hit | hit | hit |
| 7,7 | sp | sp | sp | sp | sp | sp | hit | hit | sur | sur |
| 8,8 | sp | sp | sp | sp | sp | sp | sp | sp | sur& | sur& |
| 9,9 | sp | sp | sp | sp | sp | st | sp | sp | st | st |
| 10,10 | st | st | st | st | st | st | st | st | st | st |
| A,A | sp | sp | sp | sp | sp | sp | sp | sp | sp | sp |

# CHART 39

One deck

Dealer stands on soft 17

Double down on 10 and 11 only

Doubling down after splitting is allowed

**Hard count** **Dealer's Up Card**

| Your Hand | 2 | 3 | 4 | 5 | 6 | 7 | 8 | 9 | 10 | A |
|---|---|---|---|---|---|---|---|---|---|---|
| 5 | hit | hit | hit | hit | hit | hit | hit | hit | hit | hit |
| 6 | hit | hit | hit | hit | hit | hit | hit | hit | hit | hit |
| 7 | hit | hit | hit | hit | hit | hit | hit | hit | hit | hit |
| 8 | hit | hit | hit | hit | hit | hit | hit | hit | hit | hit |
| 9 | hit | hit | hit | hit | hit | hit | hit | hit | hit | hit |
| 10 | dd | dd | dd | dd | dd | dd | dd | dd | hit | hit |
| 11 | dd | dd | dd | dd | dd | dd | dd | dd | dd | dd |
| 12 | hit | hit | st | st | st | hit | hit | hit | hit | hit |
| 13 | st | st | st | st | st | hit | hit | hit | hit | sur |

| | | | | | | | | | | |
|---|---|---|---|---|---|---|---|---|---|---|
| 14 | st | st | st | st | st | hit | hit | hit | sur | sur |
| 15 | st | st | st | st | st | hit | hit | hit | sur | sur |
| 16 | st | st | st | st | st | hit | hit | sur | sur | sur |
| 17–21 | st | st | st | st | st | st | st | st | st | st |

| **Soft Count** | | | **Dealer's Up Card** | | | | | | | |
|---|---|---|---|---|---|---|---|---|---|---|
| Your Hand | 2 | 3 | 4 | 5 | 6 | 7 | 8 | 9 | 10 | A |
| soft 13 | hit | hit | hit | hit | hit | hit | hit | hit | hit | hit |
| soft 14 | hit | hit | hit | hit | hit | hit | hit | hit | hit | hit |
| soft 15 | hit | hit | hit | hit | hit | hit | hit | hit | hit | hit |
| soft 16 | hit | hit | hit | hit | hit | hit | hit | hit | hit | hit |
| soft 17 | hit | hit | hit | hit | hit | hit | hit | hit | hit | hit |
| soft 18 | st | st | st | st | st | st | st | hit | hit | st |
| soft 19,20 | st | st | st | st | st | st | st | st | st | st |

| **Pairs** | | | **Dealer's Up Card** | | | | | | | |
|---|---|---|---|---|---|---|---|---|---|---|
| Your Hand | 2 | 3 | 4 | 5 | 6 | 7 | 8 | 9 | 10 | A |
| 2,2 | sp | sp | sp | sp | sp | sp | hit | hit | hit | hit |
| 3,3 | sp | sp | sp | sp | sp | sp | sp | hit | hit | hit |
| 4,4 | hit | hit | sp | sp | sp | hit | hit | hit | hit | hit |
| 5,5 | dd | dd | dd | dd | dd | dd | dd | dd | hit | hit |
| 6,6 | sp | sp | sp | sp | sp | sp | hit | hit | hit | hit |
| 7,7 | sp | sp | sp | sp | sp | sp | sp | hit | sur | sur |
| 8,8 | sp | sp | sp | sp | sp | sp | sp | sp | sur& | sur& |
| 9,9 | sp | sp | sp | sp | sp | st | sp | sp | st | st |
| 10,10 | st | st | st | st | st | st | st | st | st | st |
| A,A | sp | sp | sp | sp | sp | sp | sp | sp | sp | sp |

# CHART 40

One deck

Dealer stands on soft 17

Double down on 10 and 11 only

No doubling down after splitting

**Hard count**                         **Dealer's Up Card**

| Your Hand | 2 | 3 | 4 | 5 | 6 | 7 | 8 | 9 | 10 | A |
|---|---|---|---|---|---|---|---|---|---|---|
| 5 | hit | hit | hit | hit | hit | hit | hit | hit | hit | hit |
| 6 | hit | hit | hit | hit | hit | hit | hit | hit | hit | hit |
| 7 | hit | hit | hit | hit | hit | hit | hit | hit | hit | hit |
| 8 | hit | hit | hit | hit | hit | hit | hit | hit | hit | hit |
| 9 | hit | hit | hit | hit | hit | hit | hit | hit | hit | hit |
| 10 | dd | dd | dd | dd | dd | dd | dd | dd | hit | hit |
| 11 | dd | dd | dd | dd | dd | dd | dd | dd | dd | dd |
| 12 | hit | hit | st | st | st | hit | hit | hit | hit | hit |
| 13 | st | st | st | st | st | hit | hit | hit | hit | sur |
| 14 | st | st | st | st | st | hit | hit | hit | sur | sur |
| 15 | st | st | st | st | st | hit | hit | hit | sur | sur |
| 16 | st | st | st | st | st | hit | hit | sur | sur | sur |
| 17–21 | st | st | st | st | st | st | st | st | st | st |

**Soft Count**                         **Dealer's Up Card**

| Your Hand | 2 | 3 | 4 | 5 | 6 | 7 | 8 | 9 | 10 | A |
|---|---|---|---|---|---|---|---|---|---|---|
| soft 13 | hit | hit | hit | hit | hit | hit | hit | hit | hit | hit |
| soft 14 | hit | hit | hit | hit | hit | hit | hit | hit | hit | hit |
| soft 15 | hit | hit | hit | hit | hit | hit | hit | hit | hit | hit |
| soft 16 | hit | hit | hit | hit | hit | hit | hit | hit | hit | hit |
| soft 17 | hit | hit | hit | hit | hit | hit | hit | hit | hit | hit |
| soft 18 | st | st | st | st | st | st | st | hit | hit | st |
| soft 19,20 | st | st | st | st | st | st | st | st | st | st |

**Pairs** — **Dealer's Up Card**

| Your Hand | 2 | 3 | 4 | 5 | 6 | 7 | 8 | 9 | 10 | A |
|---|---|---|---|---|---|---|---|---|---|---|
| 2,2 | hit | sp | sp | sp | sp | sp | hit | hit | hit | hit |
| 3,3 | hit | hit | sp | sp | sp | sp | hit | hit | hit | hit |
| 4,4 | hit | hit | hit | dd | dd | hit | hit | hit | hit | hit |
| 5,5 | dd | dd | dd | dd | dd | dd | dd | dd | hit | hit |
| 6,6 | sp | sp | sp | sp | sp | hit | hit | hit | hit | hit |
| 7,7 | sp | sp | sp | sp | sp | sp | hit | hit | sur | sur |
| 8,8 | sp | sp | sp | sp | sp | sp | sp | sp | sur& | sur& |
| 9,9 | sp | sp | sp | sp | sp | st | sp | sp | st | st |
| 10,10 | st | st | st | st | st | st | st | st | st | st |
| A,A | sp | sp | sp | sp | sp | sp | sp | sp | sp | sp |

# SUGGESTED READING

Griffin, Peter A. *The Theory of Blackjack.* Las Vegas, Nevada: Huntington Press, 1979.

Humble, Lance, Ph.D., and Carl Cooper, Ph.D. *The World's Greatest Blackjack Book.* New York: Doubleday, 1980.

Lembeck, Frederick. *Beat the House.* New York: Citadel Press, 1997.

Vinson, Barney. "Blackjack: The Best Game in the House." *High Roller* #1, Summer 1999, p. 16.

Revere, Lawrence. *Playing Blackjack as a Business.* Secaucus, New Jersey: Lyle Stuart, Inc., 1982.

Thorp, Edward O., Ph.D. *Beat the Dealer: A Winning Strategy for the Game of Twenty-One.* New York: Vintage Books, 1966.

Uston, Ken. *Million Dollar Blackjack.* Secaucus, New Jersey: Carol Publishing Group, 1969.

Vancura, Olaf, Ph.D., and Fuchs, Ken. *Knock-Out Blackjack.* Las Vegas, Nevada: Huntington Press, 1998.

Wong, Stanford. *Professional Blackjack.* La Jolla, California: Pi Yee Press, 1975.